I0390594

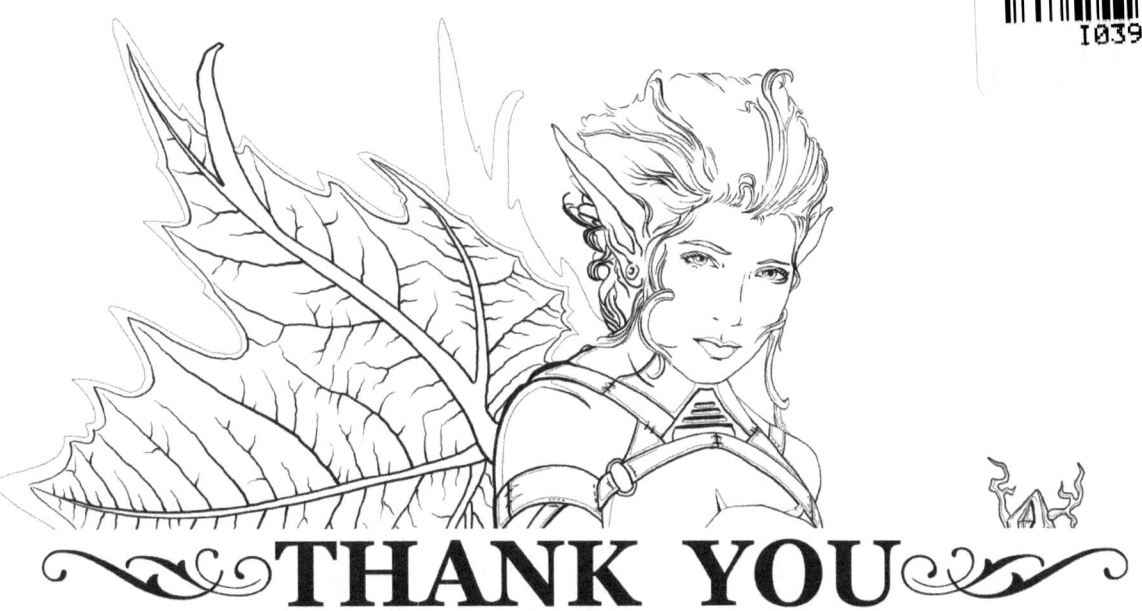

THANK YOU

I WOULD LIKE TO SAY THANK YOU TO EVERYONE THAT PURCHASED THIS
BOOK I HAVE WORKED SO HARD ON.

WITH ANY LUCK, ART OF FANTASY - VOL 1 WILL BE THE FIRST
OF MANY ADVANCED COLORING BOOKS I PLAN TO PUBLISH.

GIVE MY FACEBOOK PAGE A "LIKE" AND FEEL FREE TO POST PICTURES
OF YOUR COLORING ON MY ART. I WOULD LOVE TO SEE!

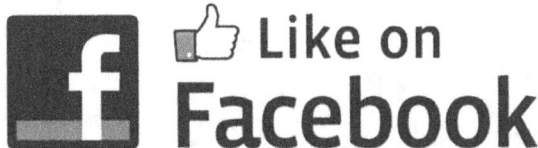

HTTPS://WWW.FACEBOOK.COM/ARTOFCARLGOOKINS

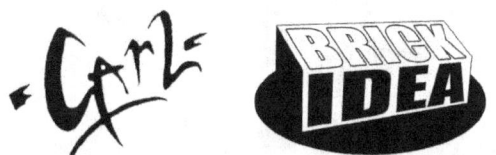

ART OF FANTASY - VOL 1 PRINT ON DEMAND EDITION
REVISION 1.0
COPYRIGHT © CARL GOOKINS - BRICK IDEA ENTERTAINMENT 2016

TEST PAGE

USE THIS PAGE TO TRY YOUR MARKERS, PENCILS, PAINTS OR CRAYONS.

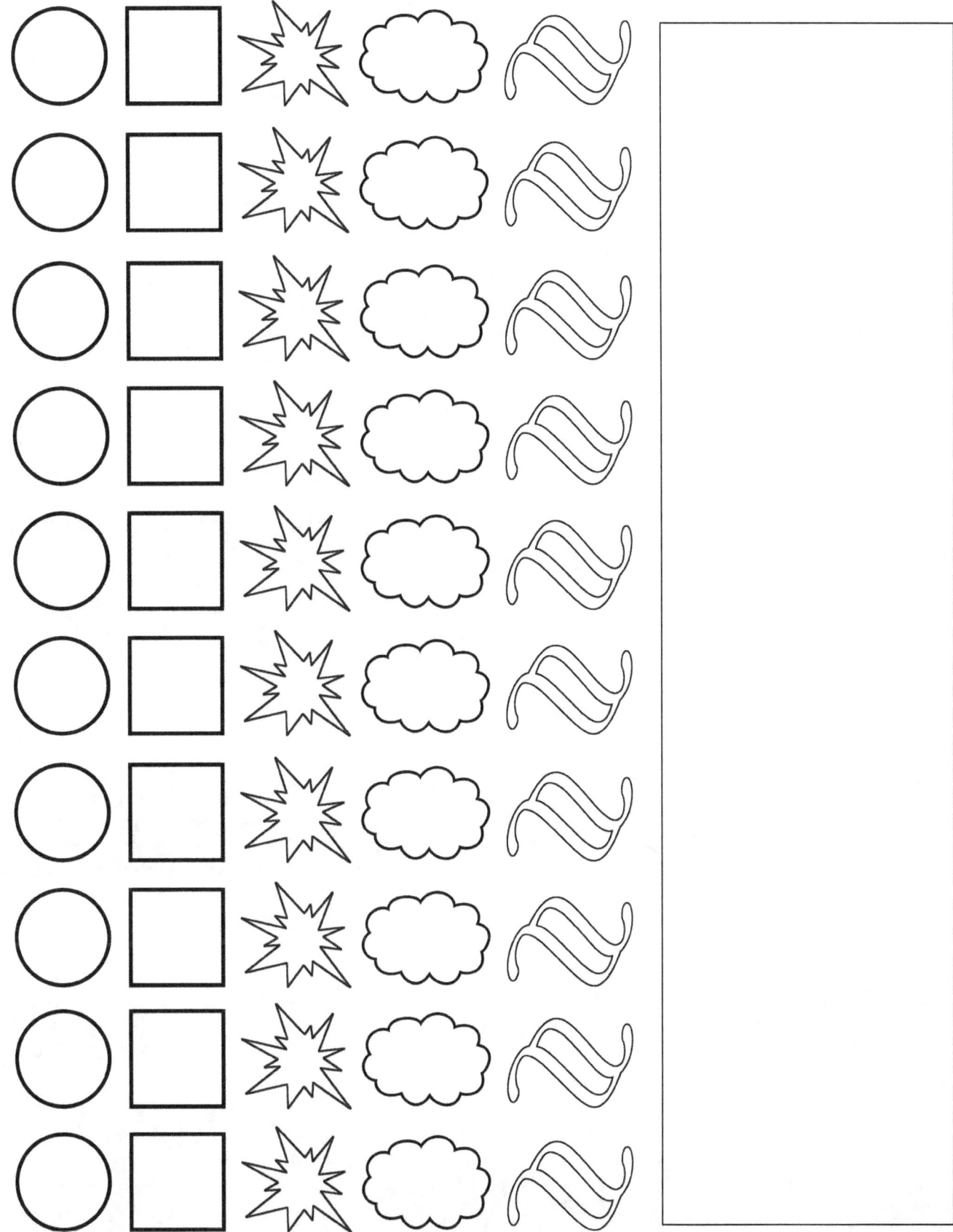

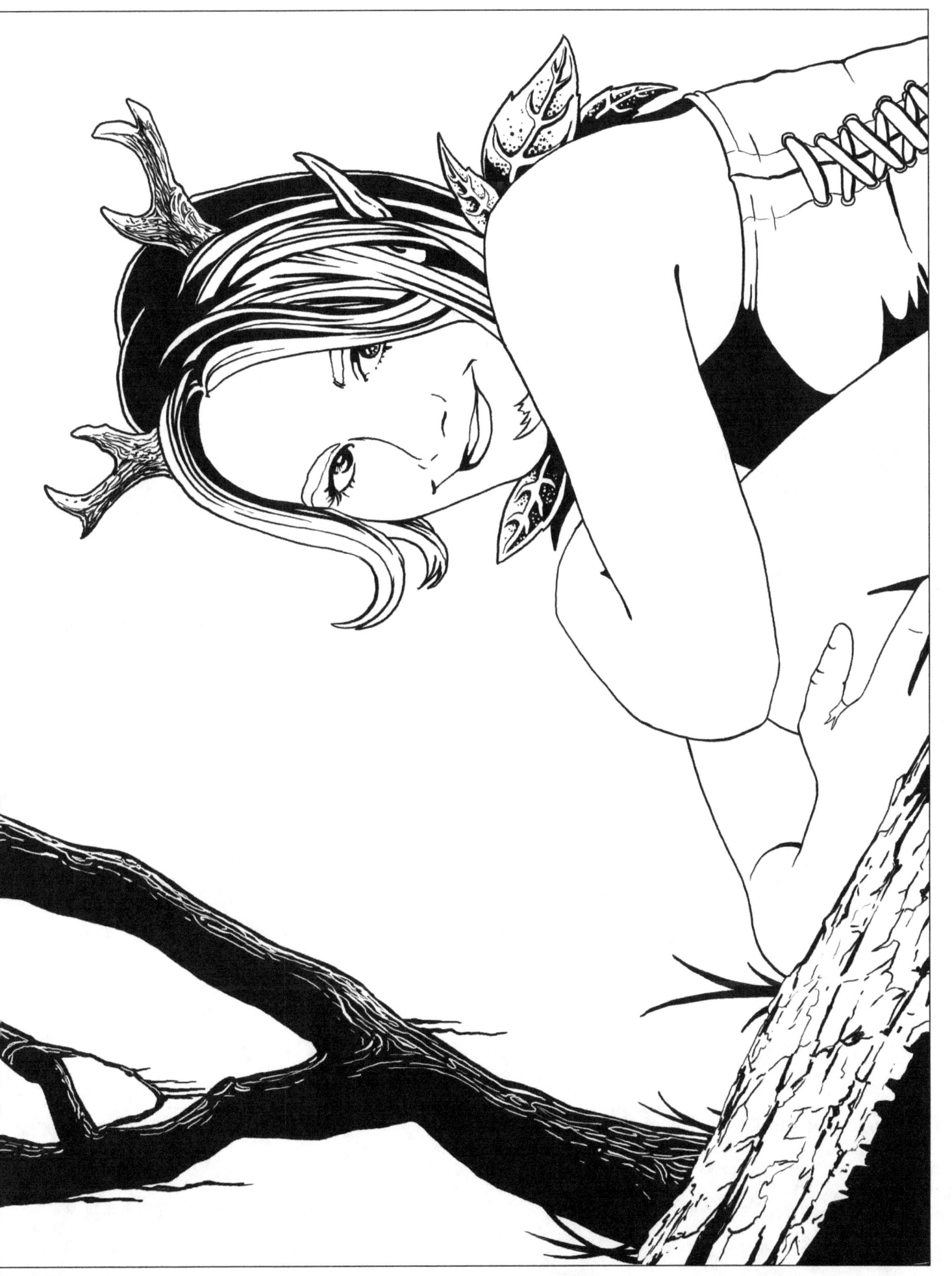

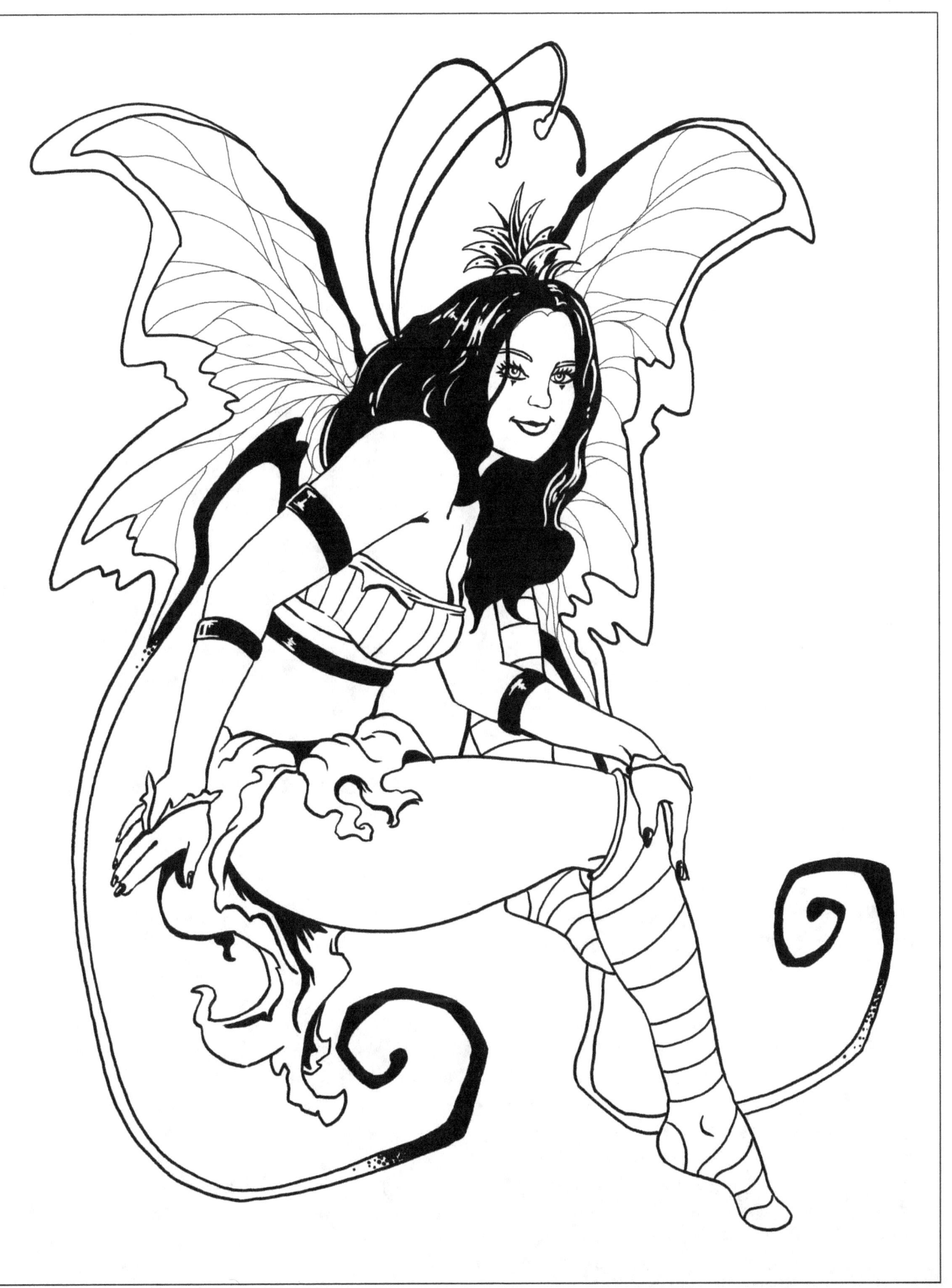

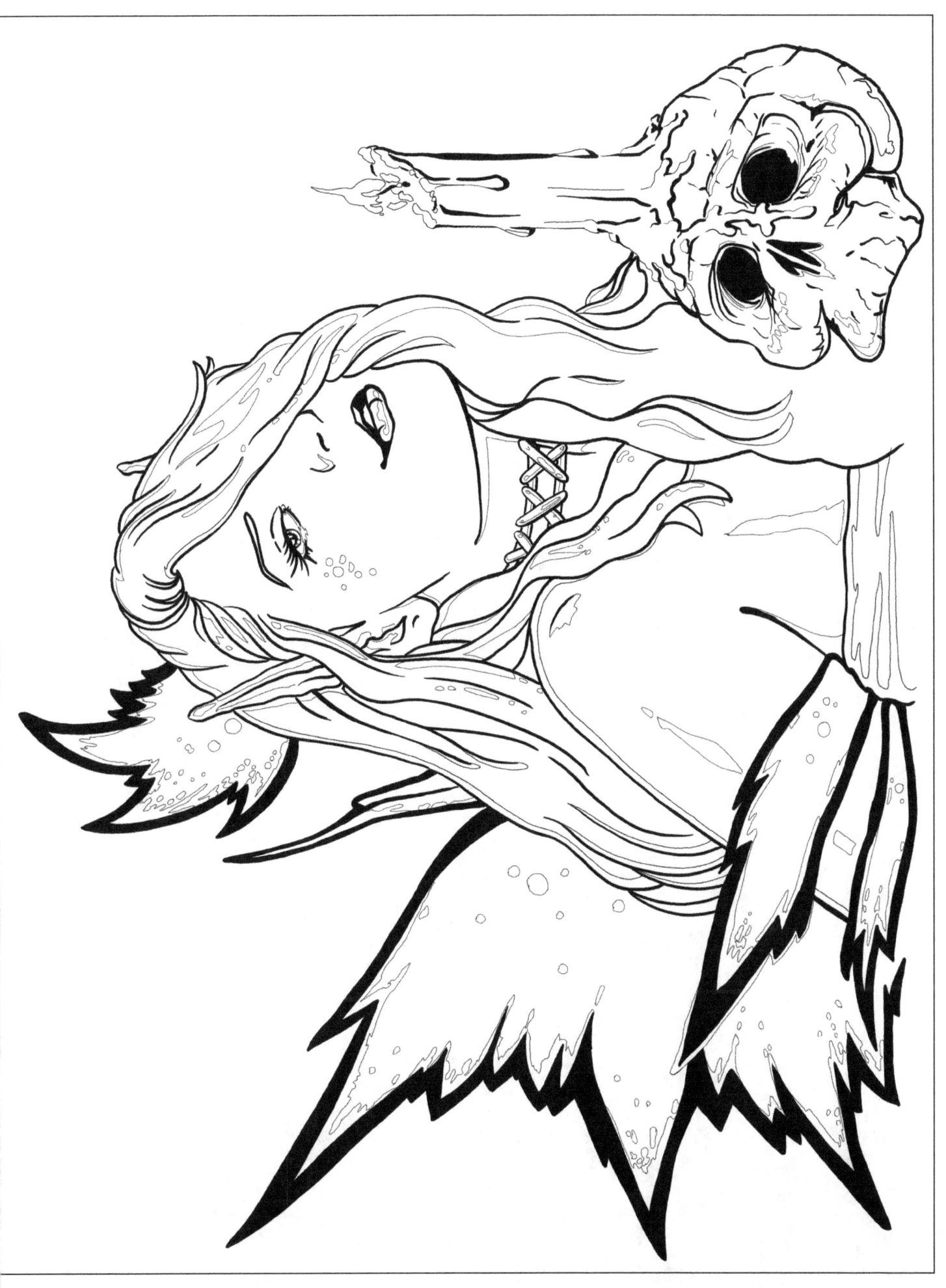

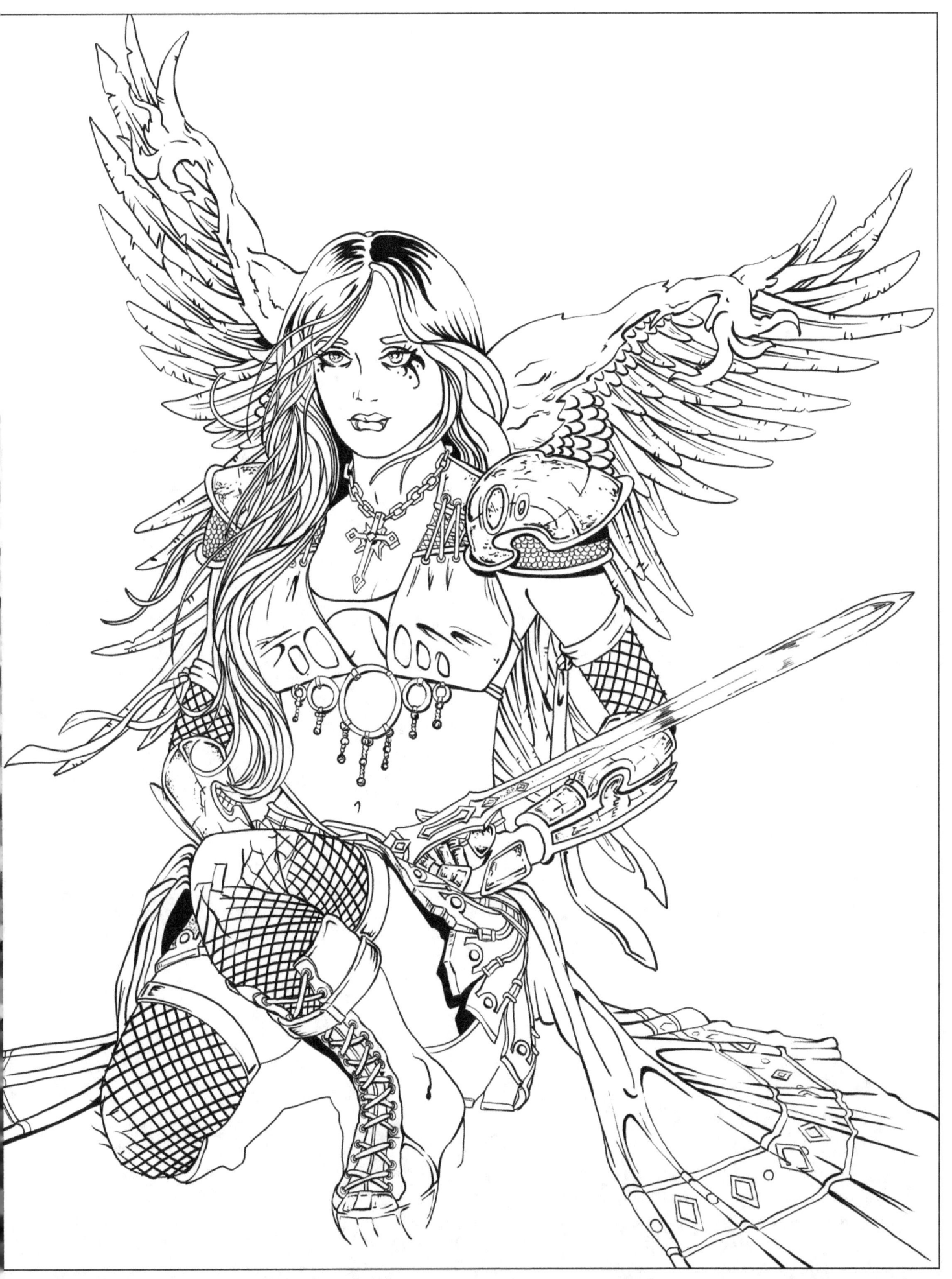

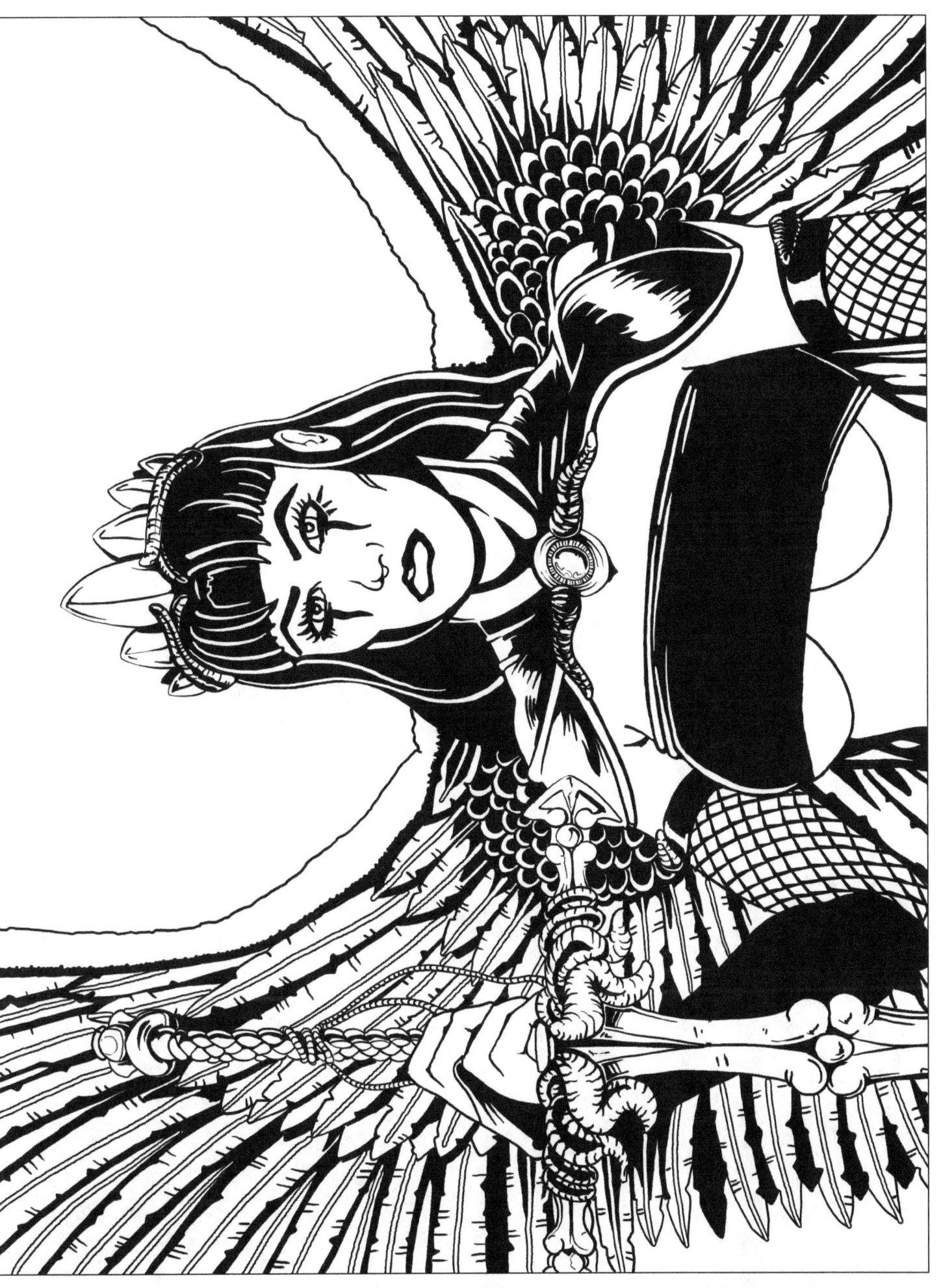

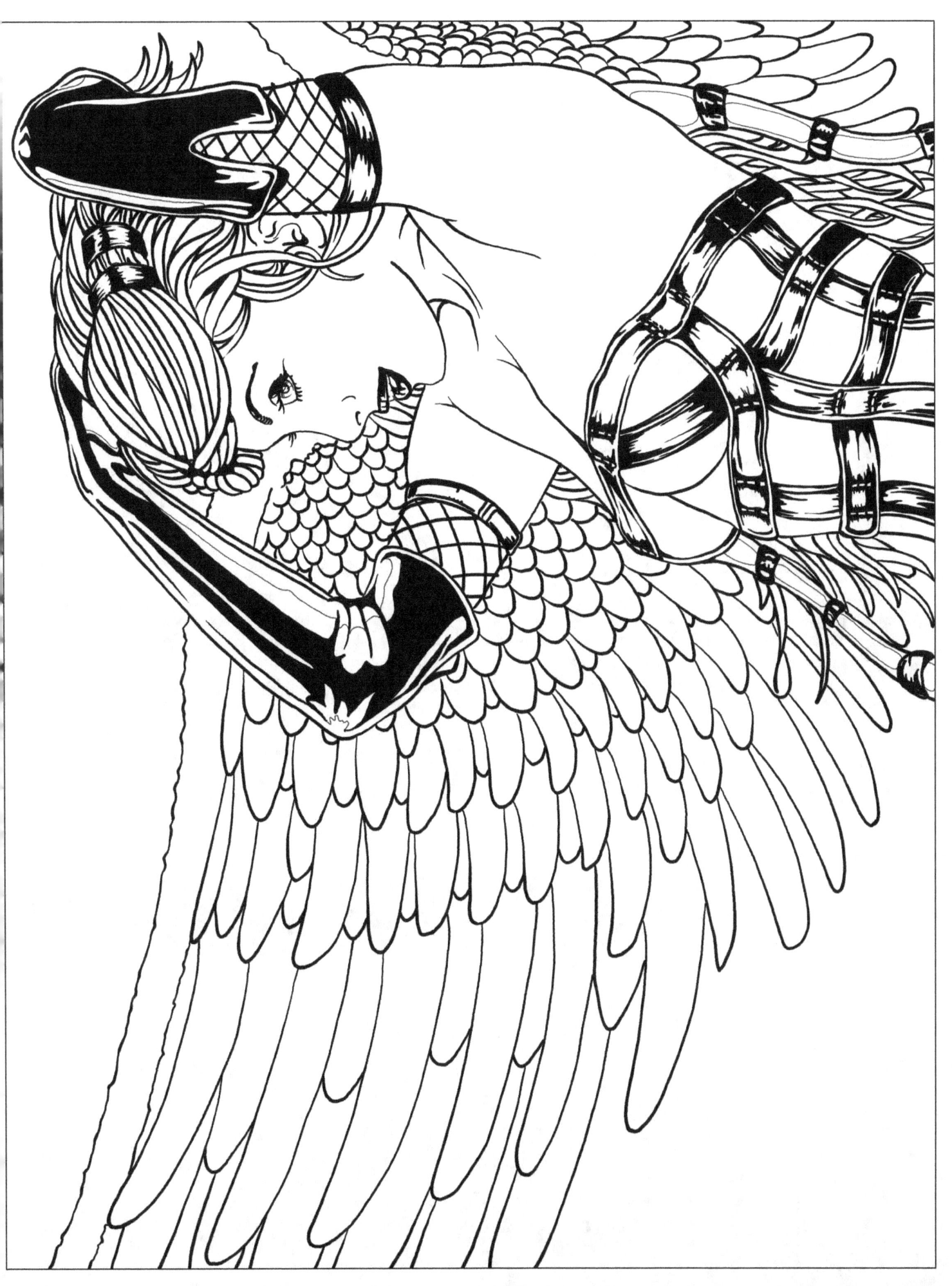

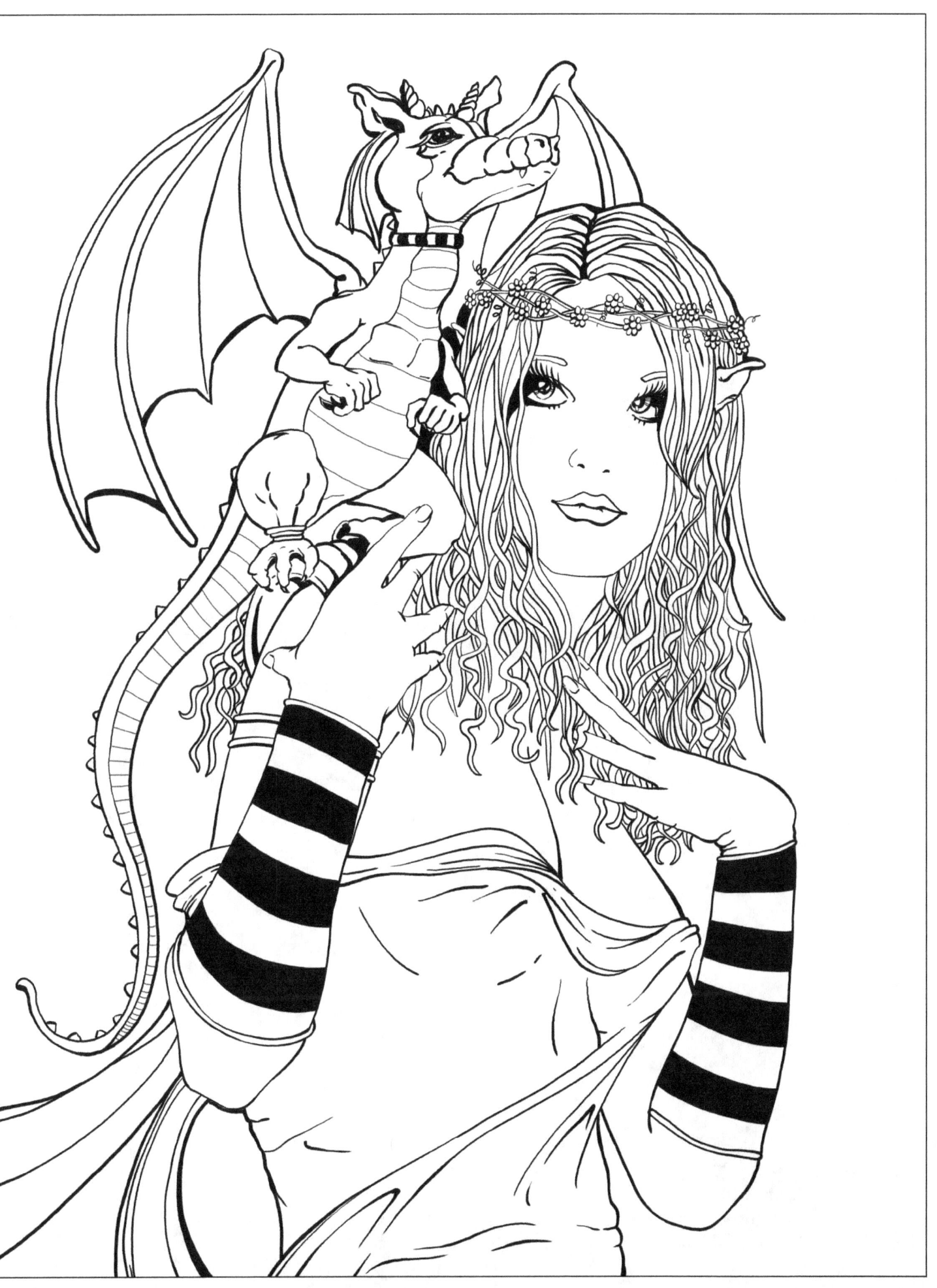

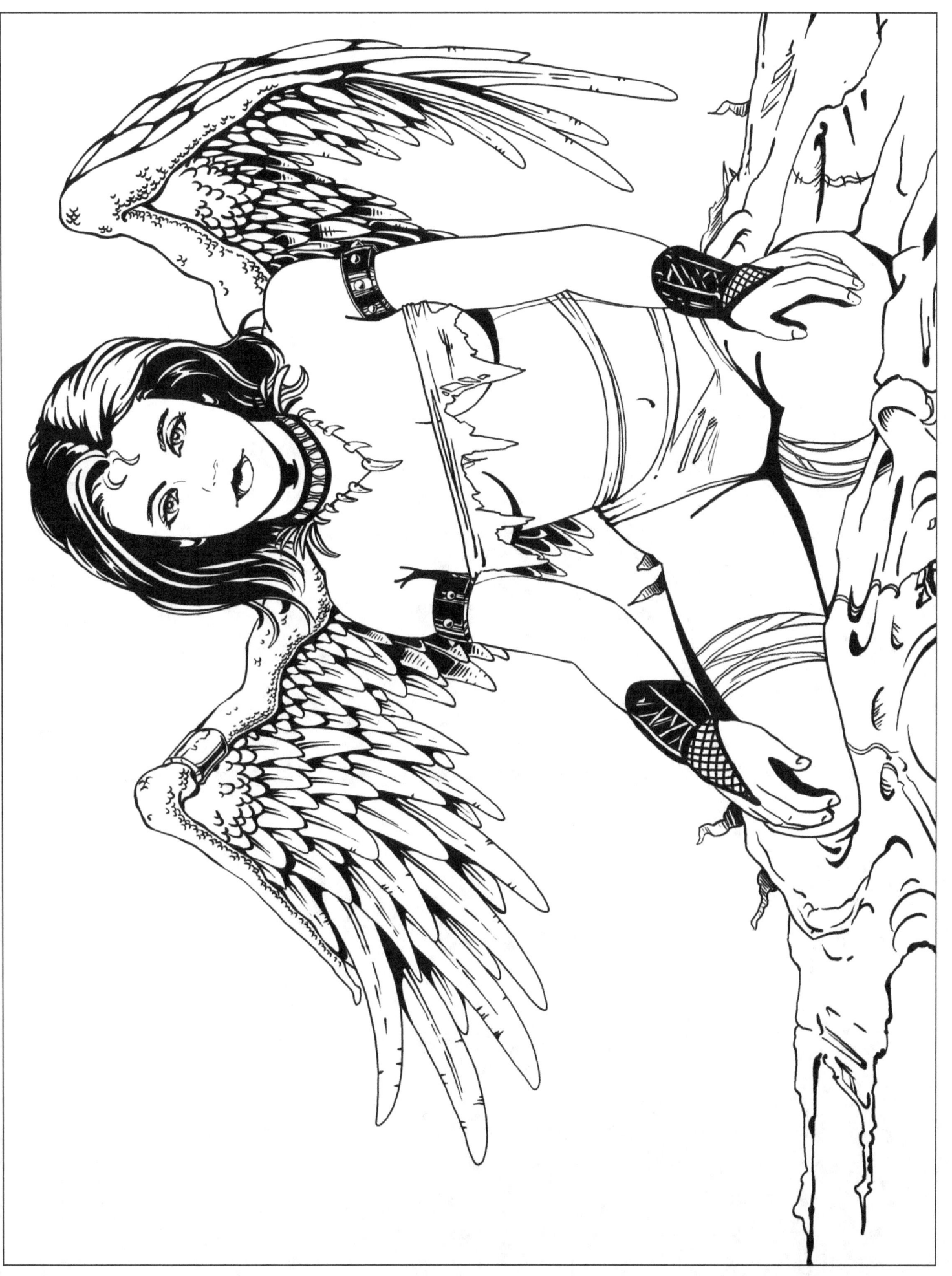

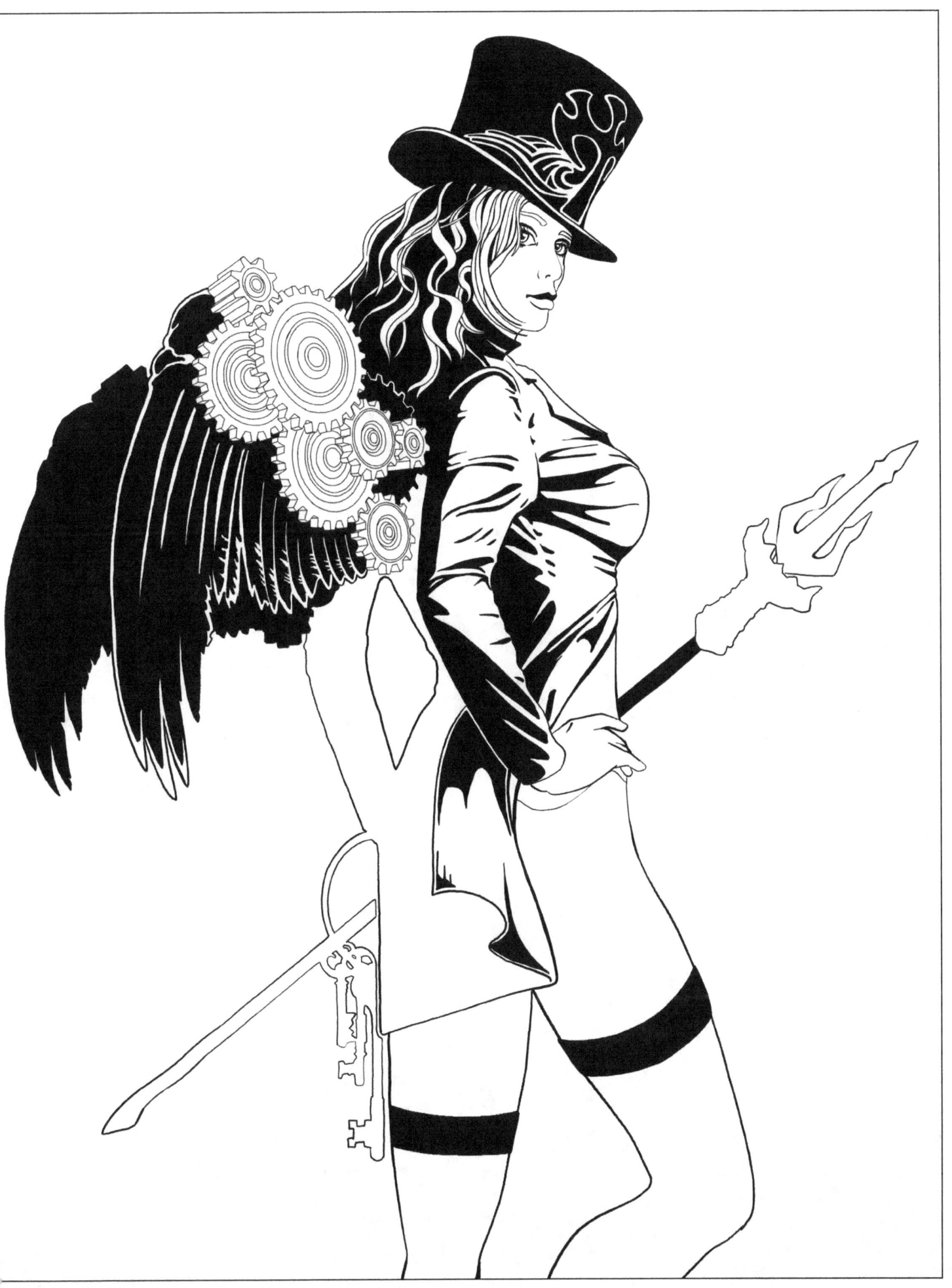

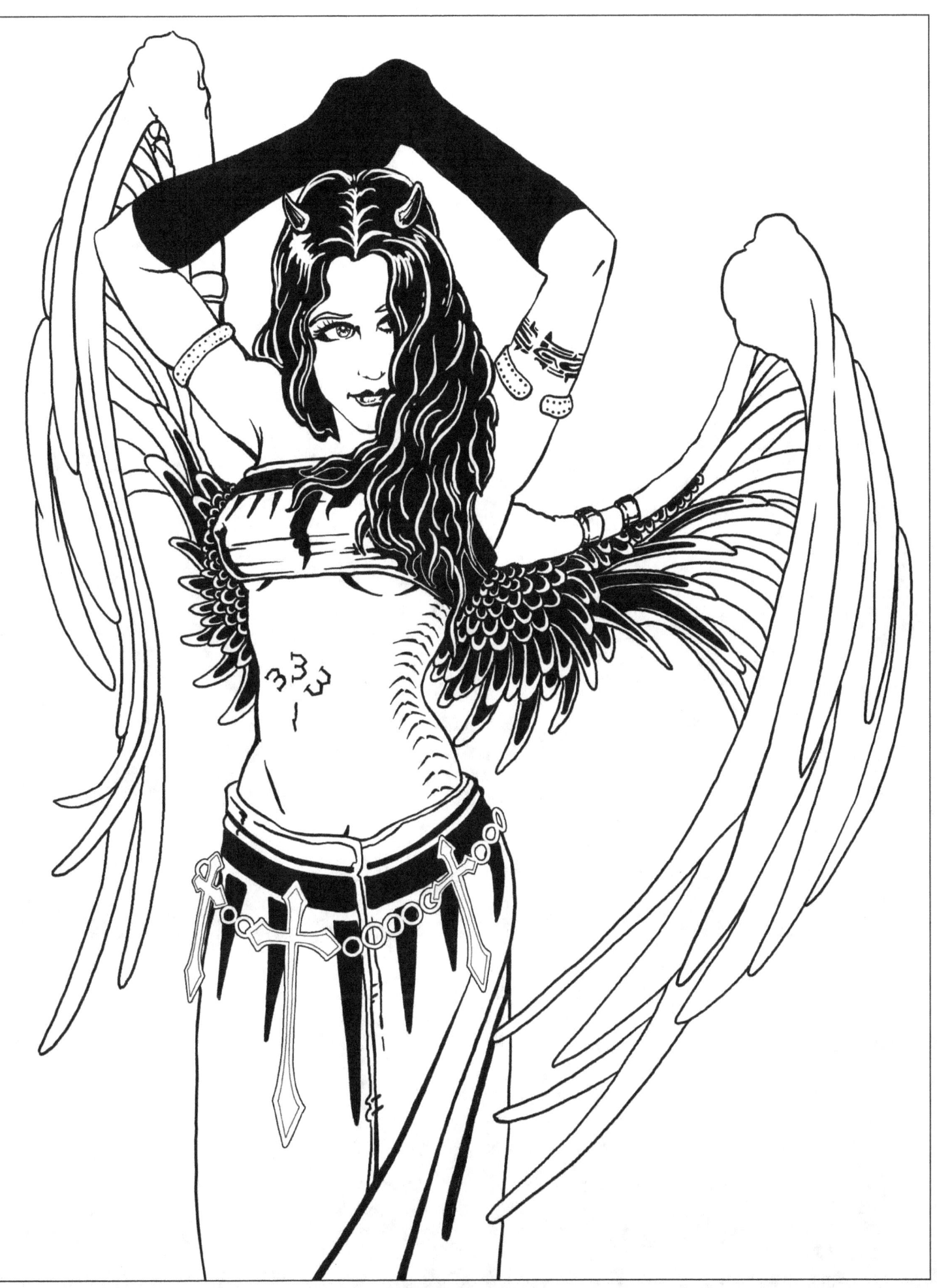

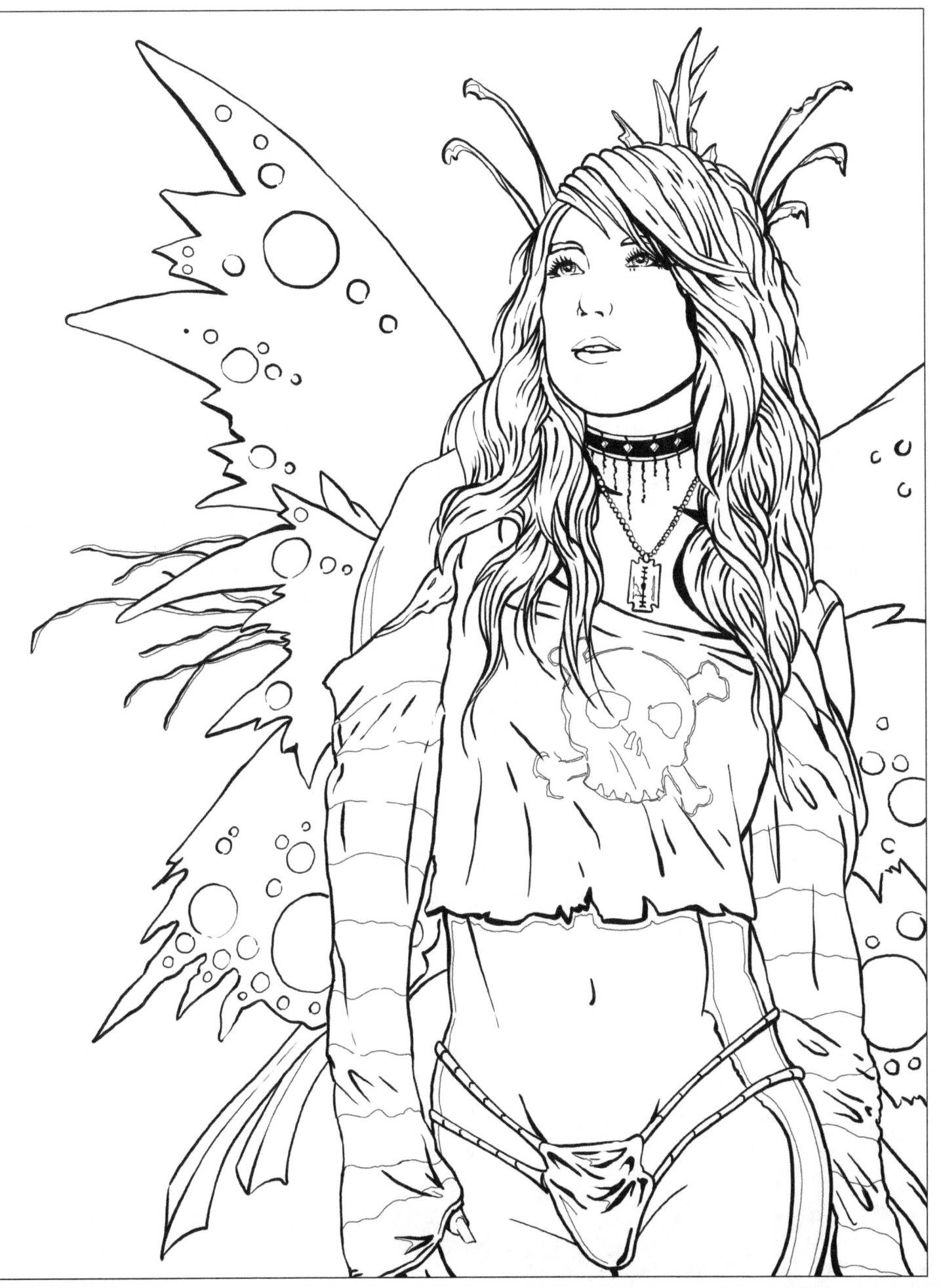

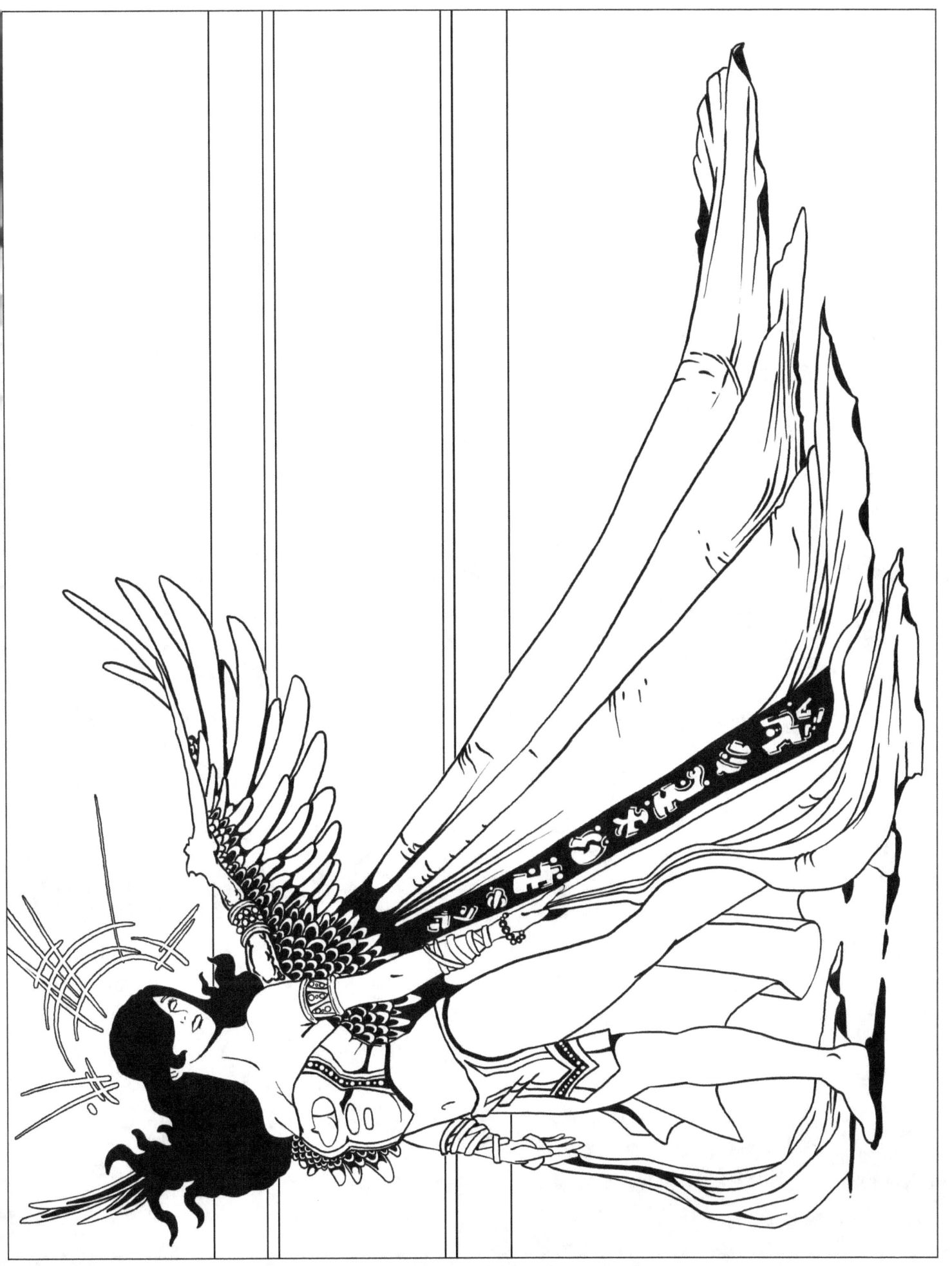

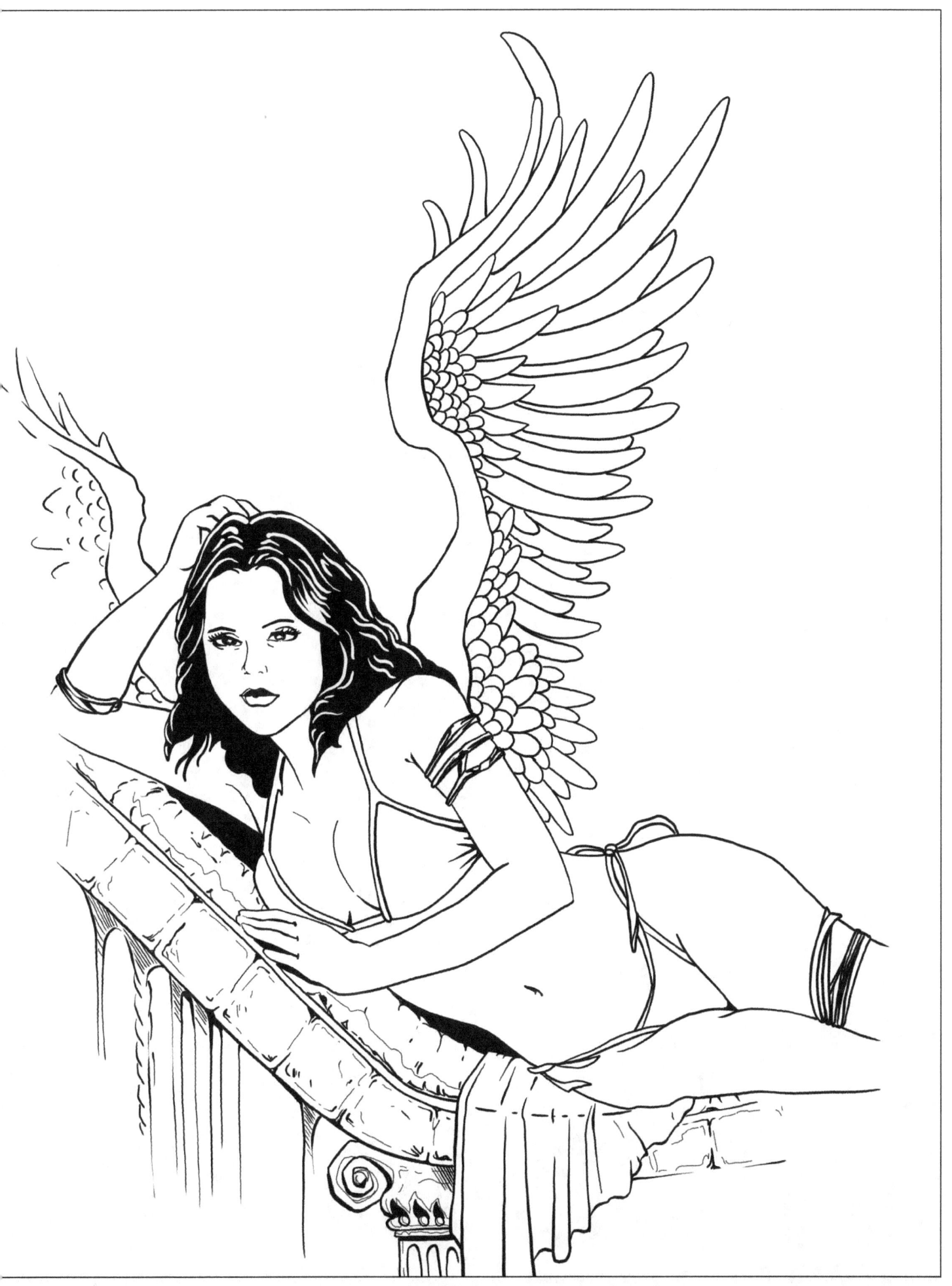

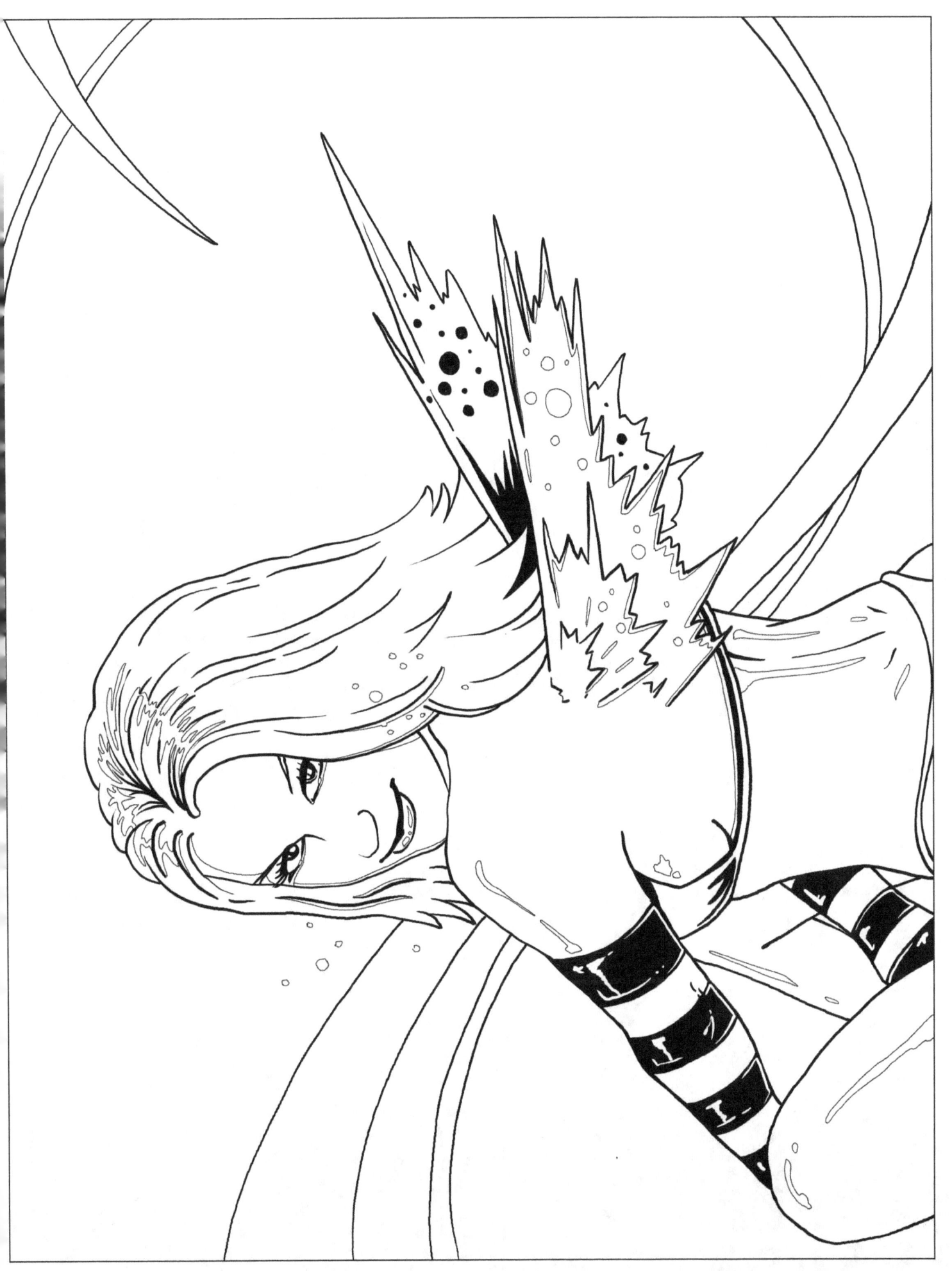

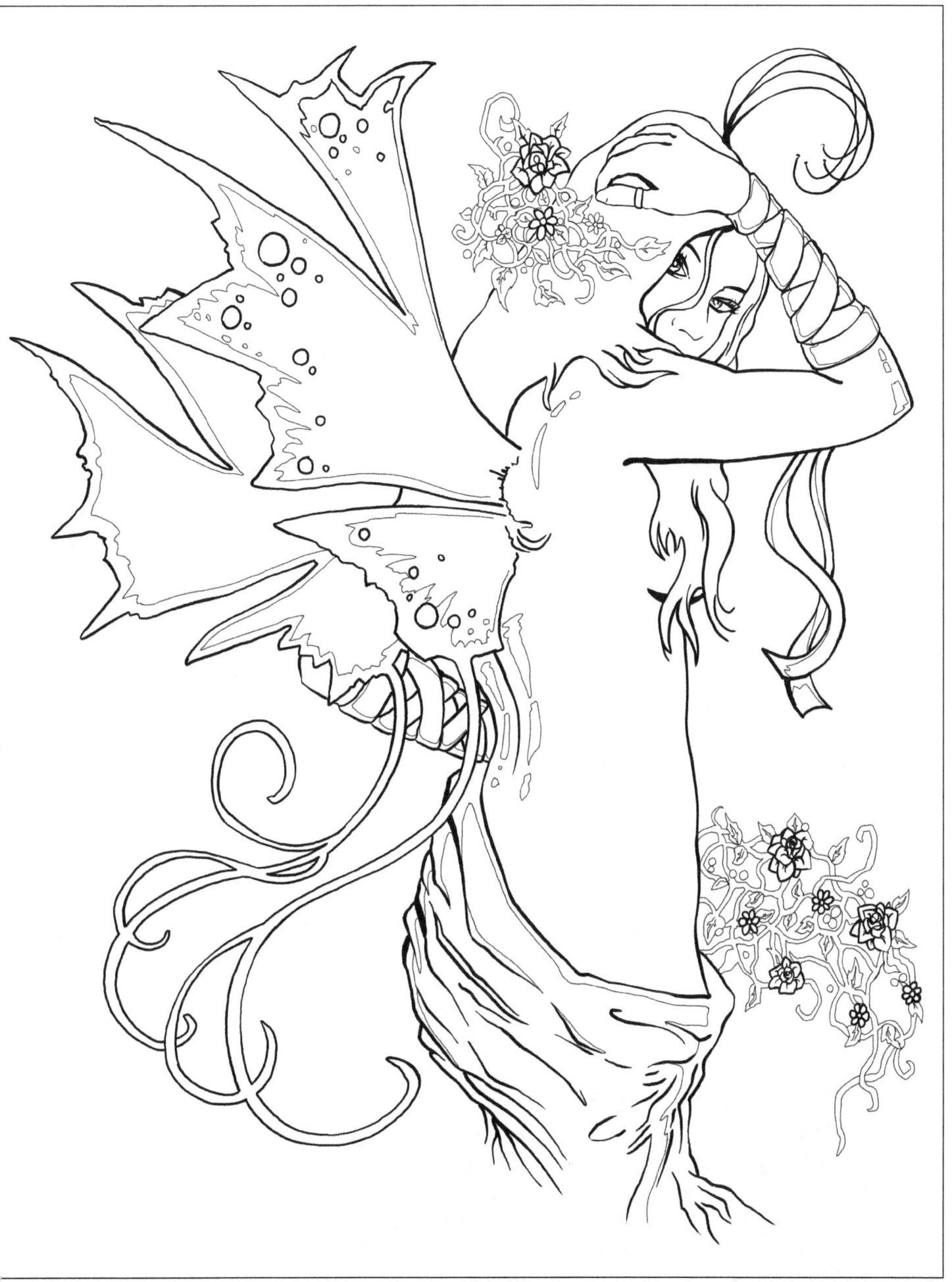

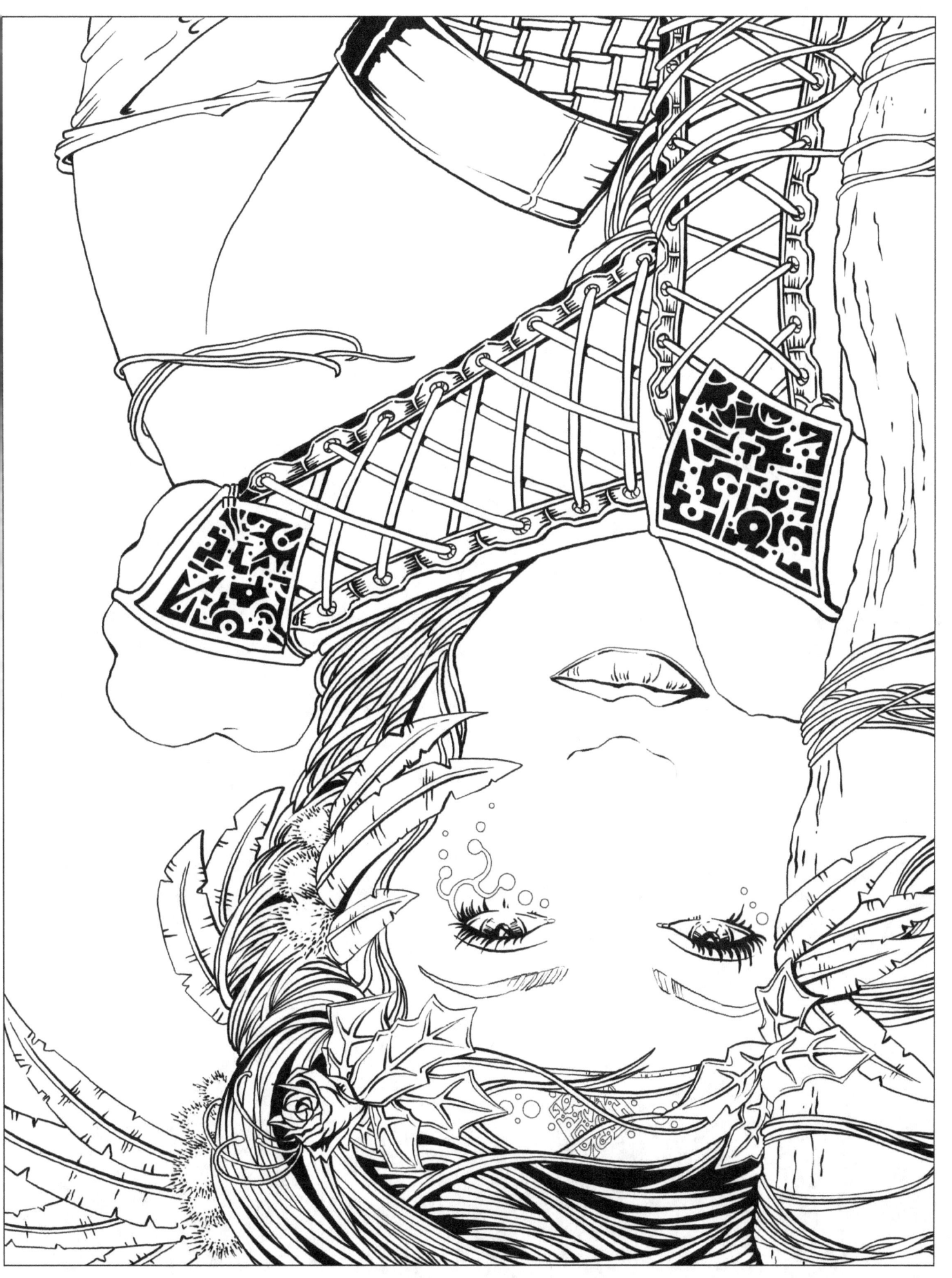

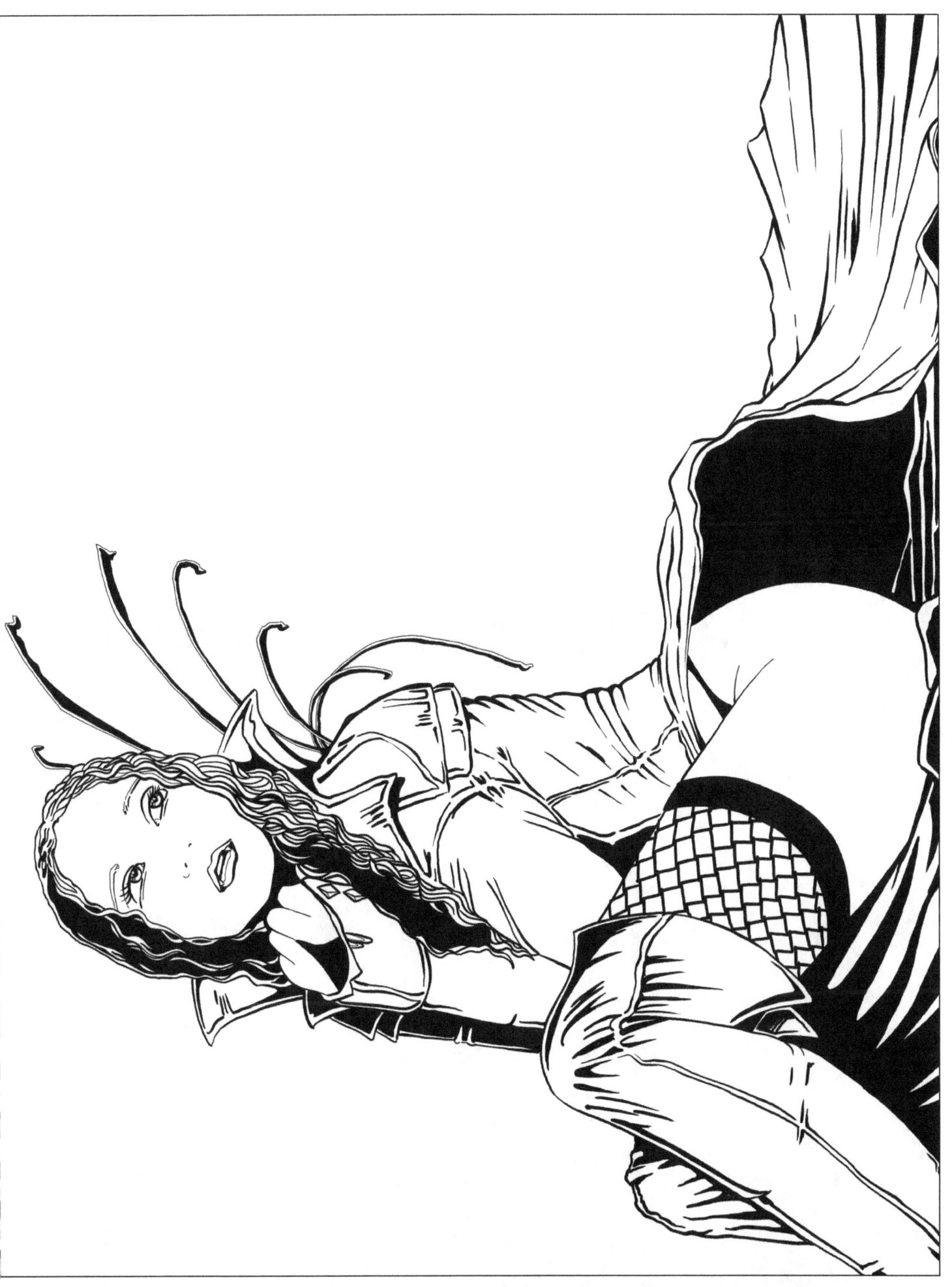

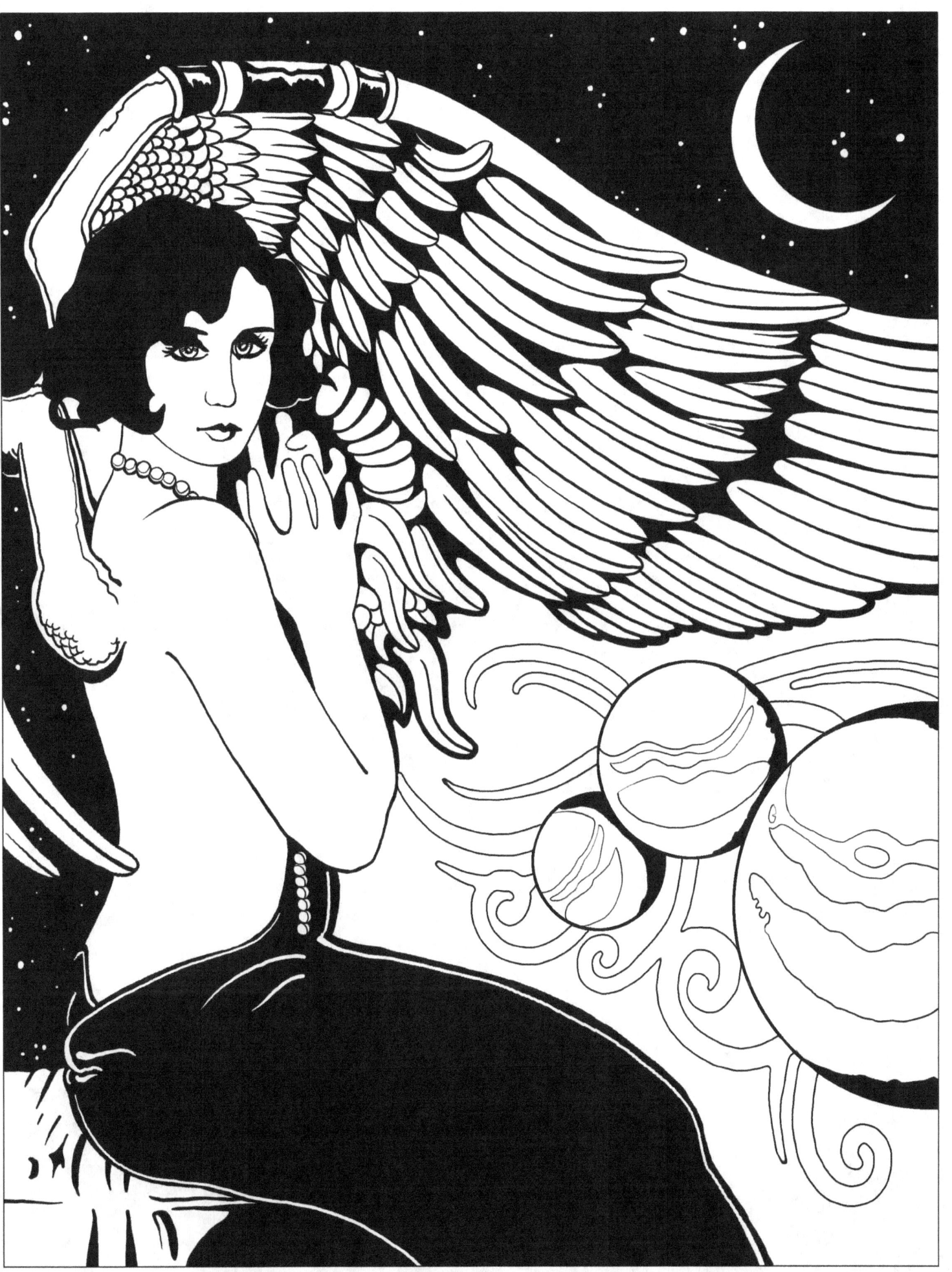

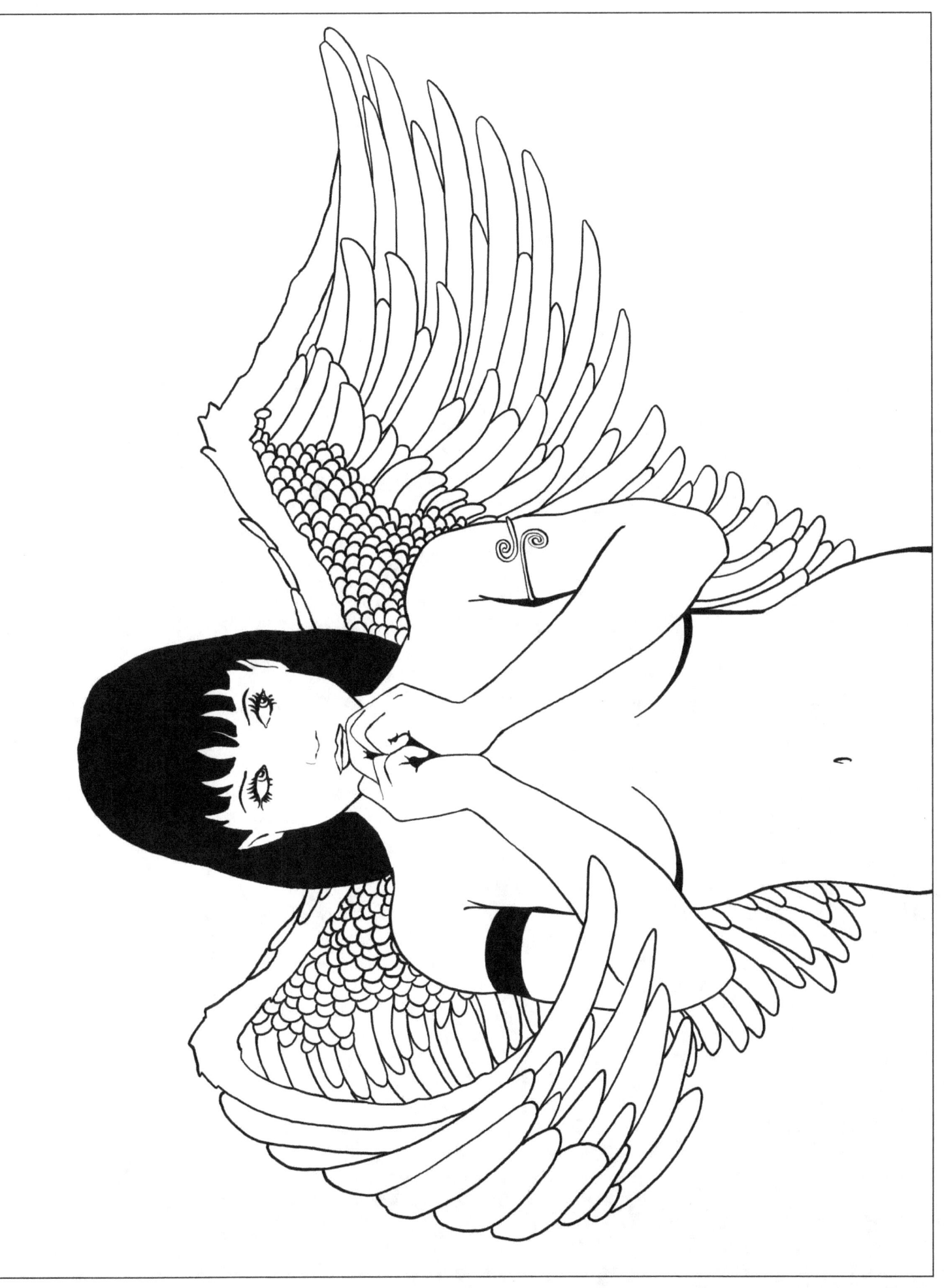

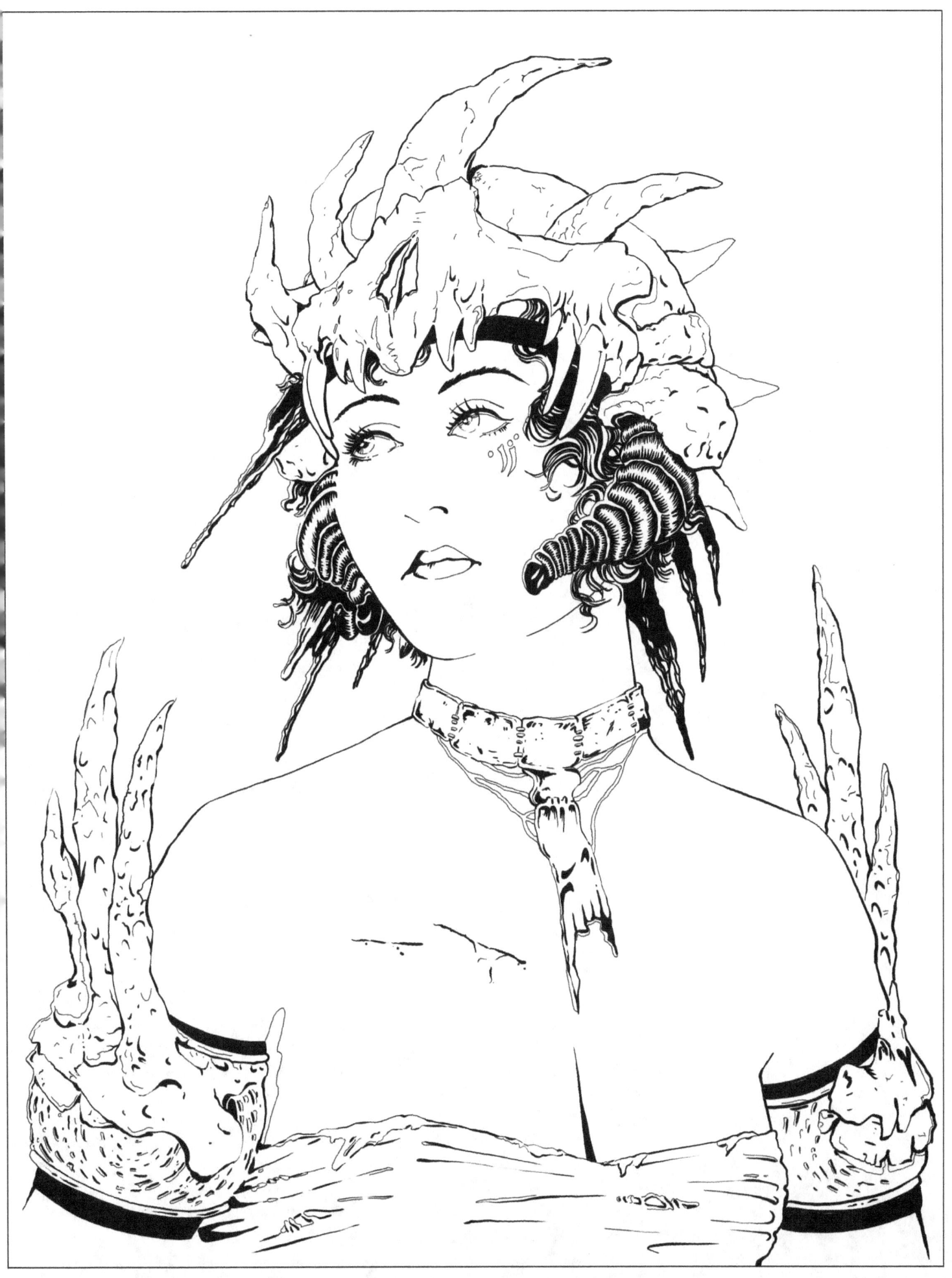

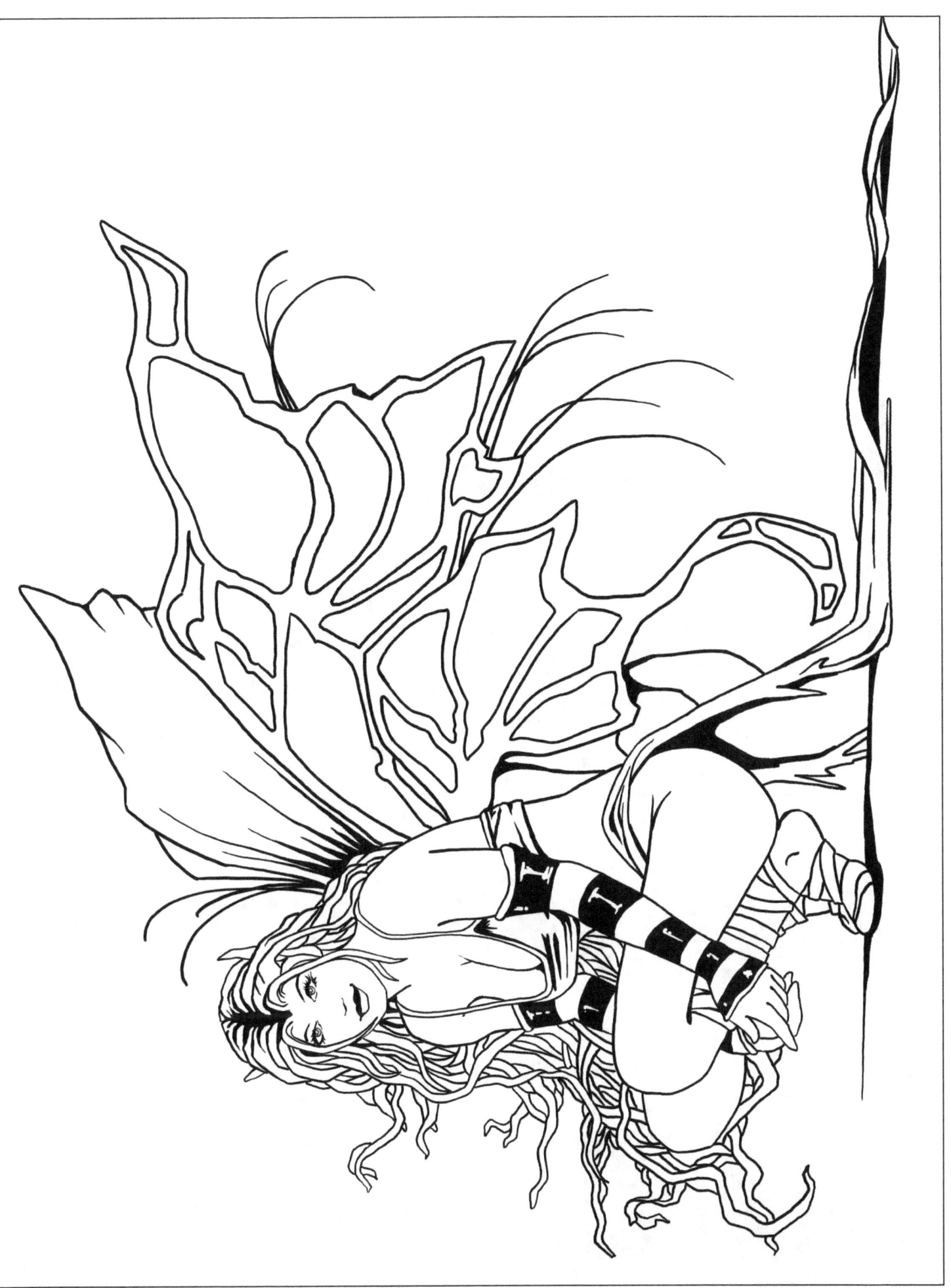

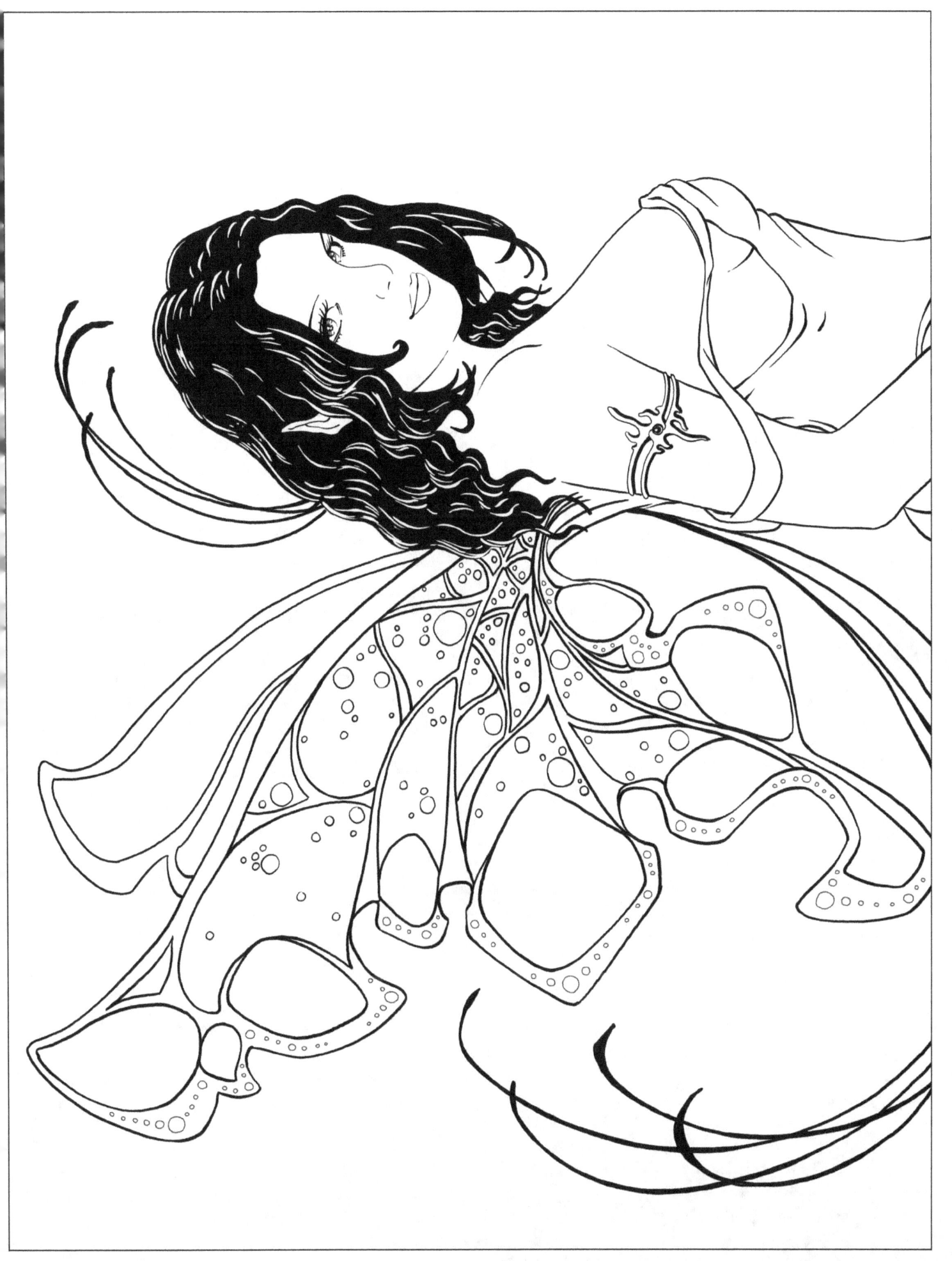

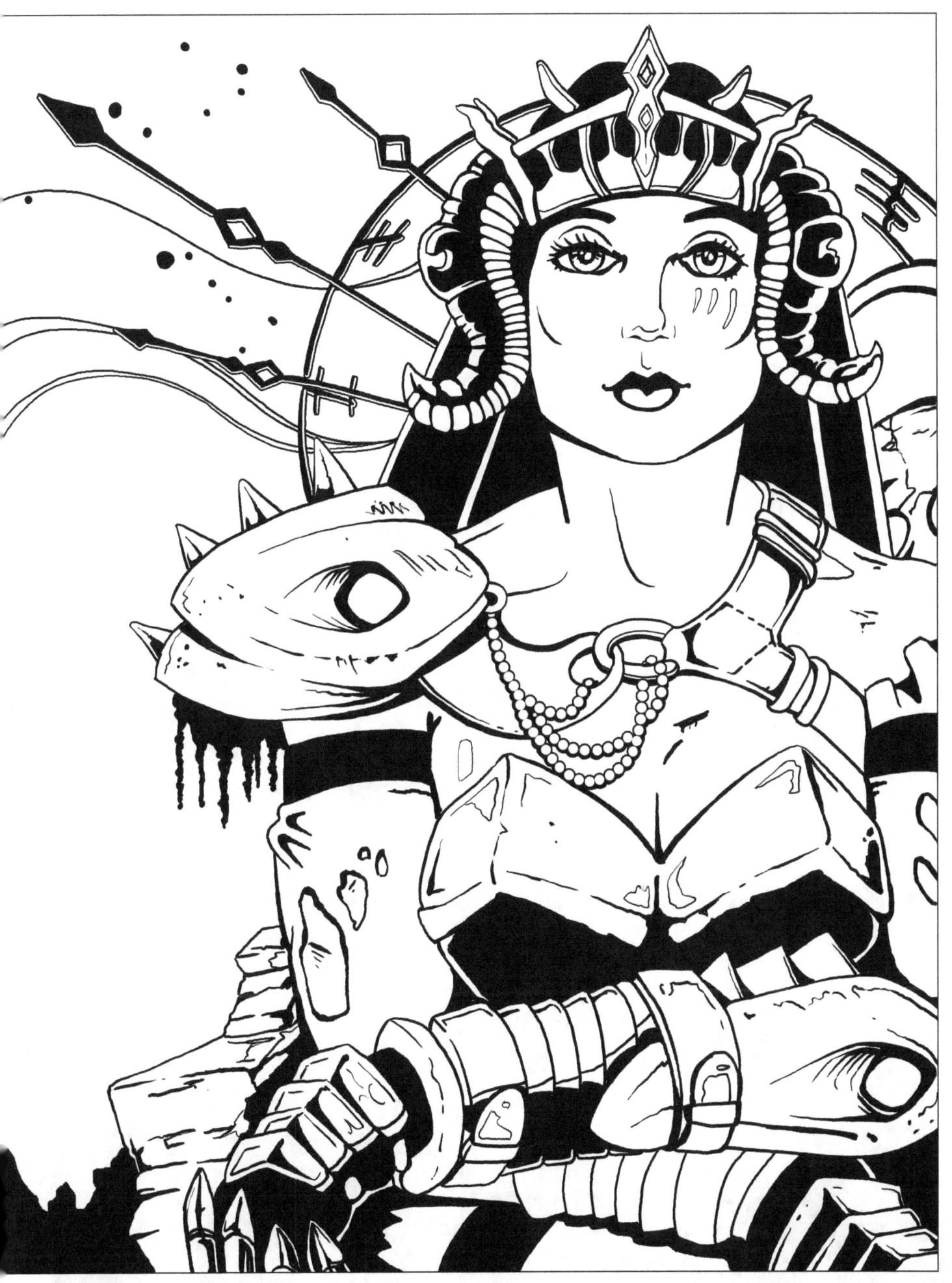

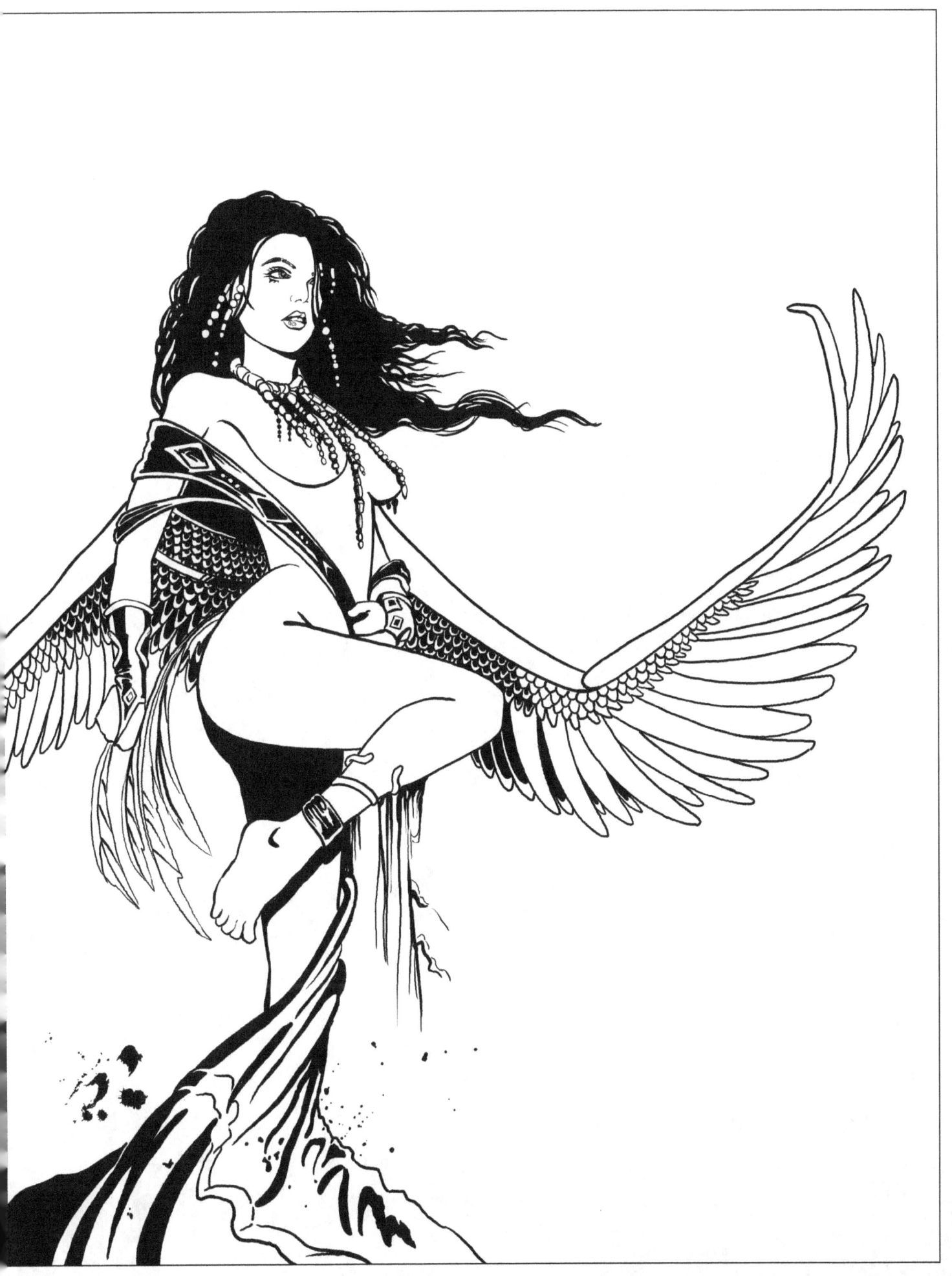

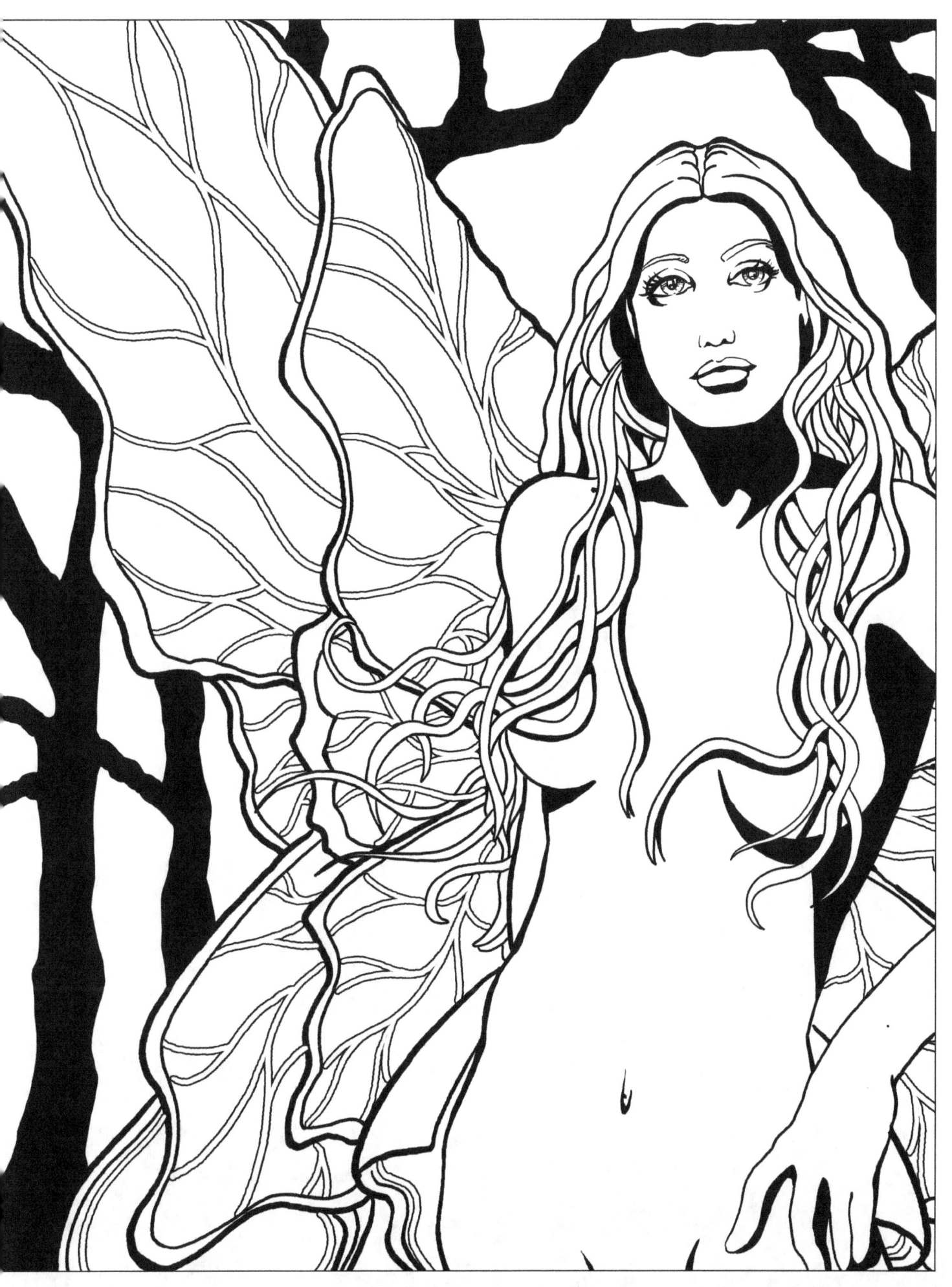

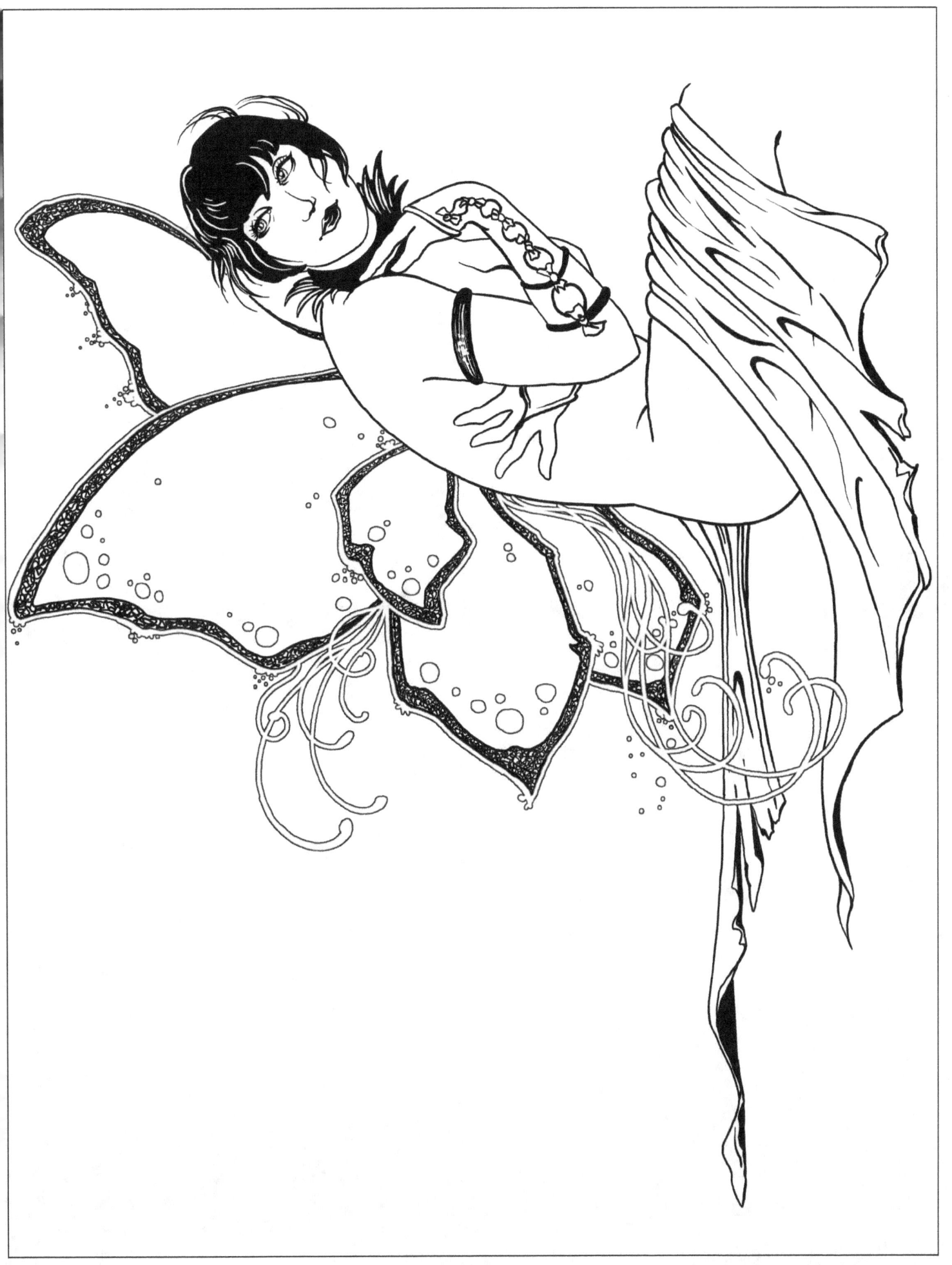

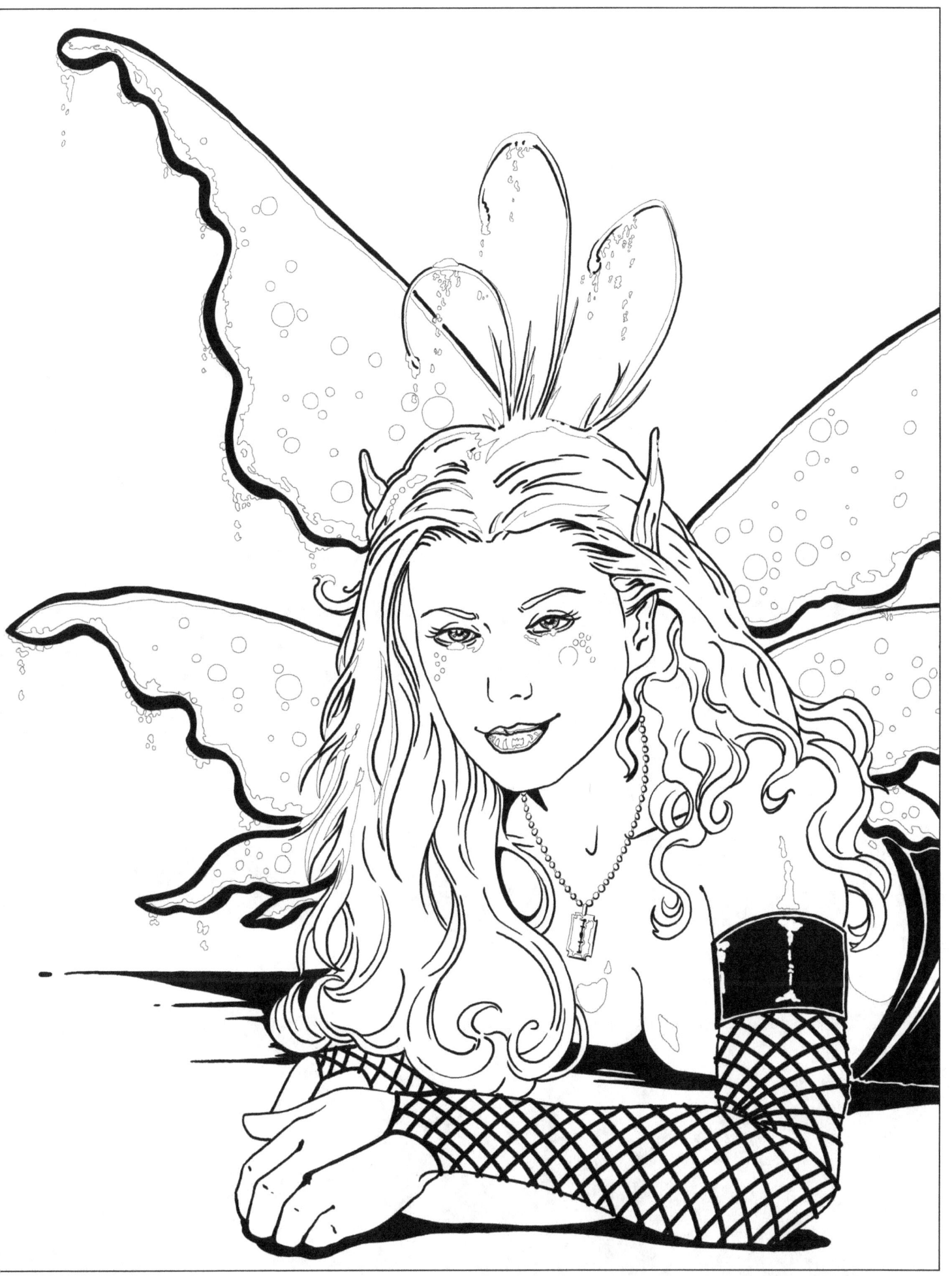

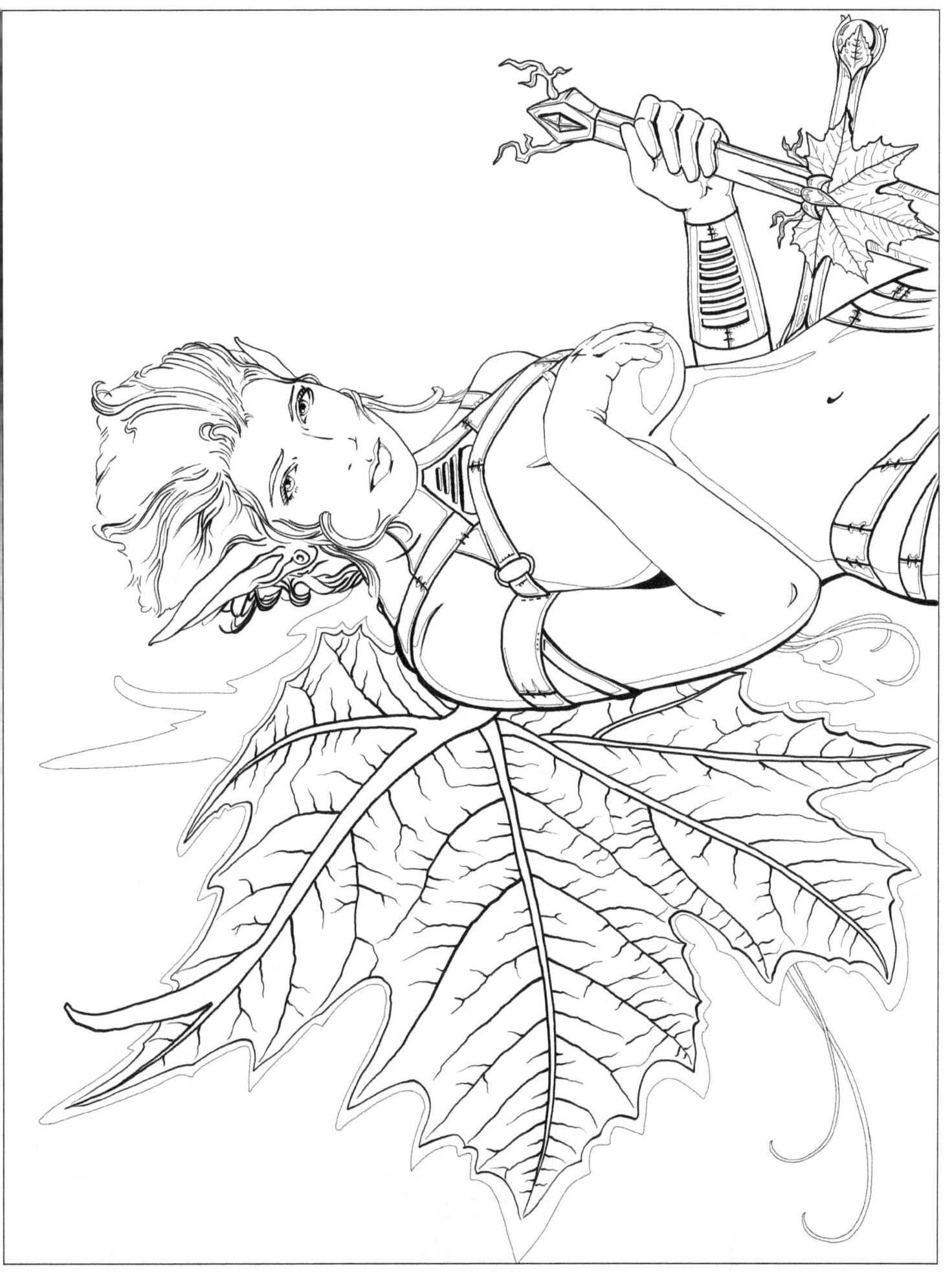

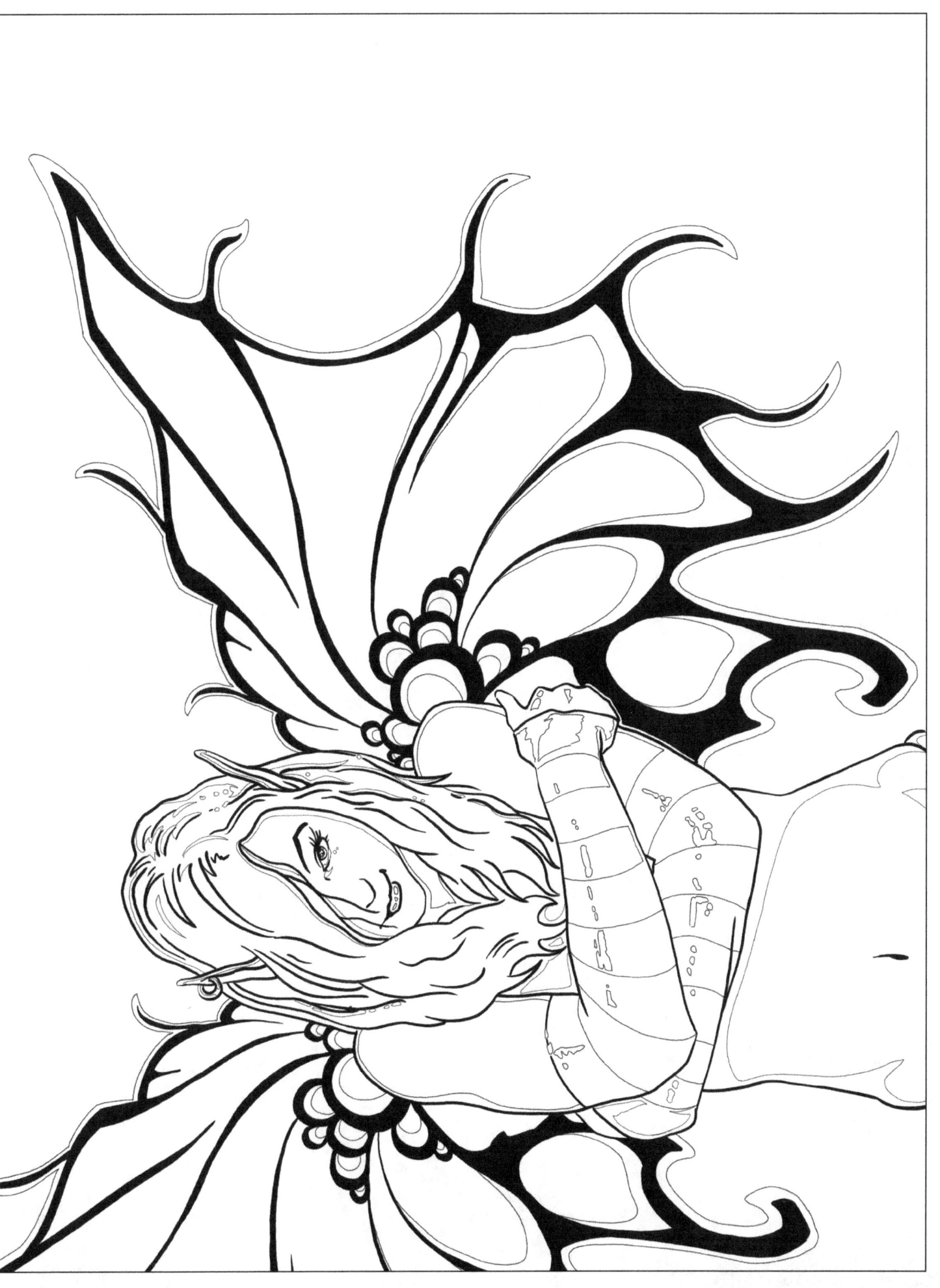

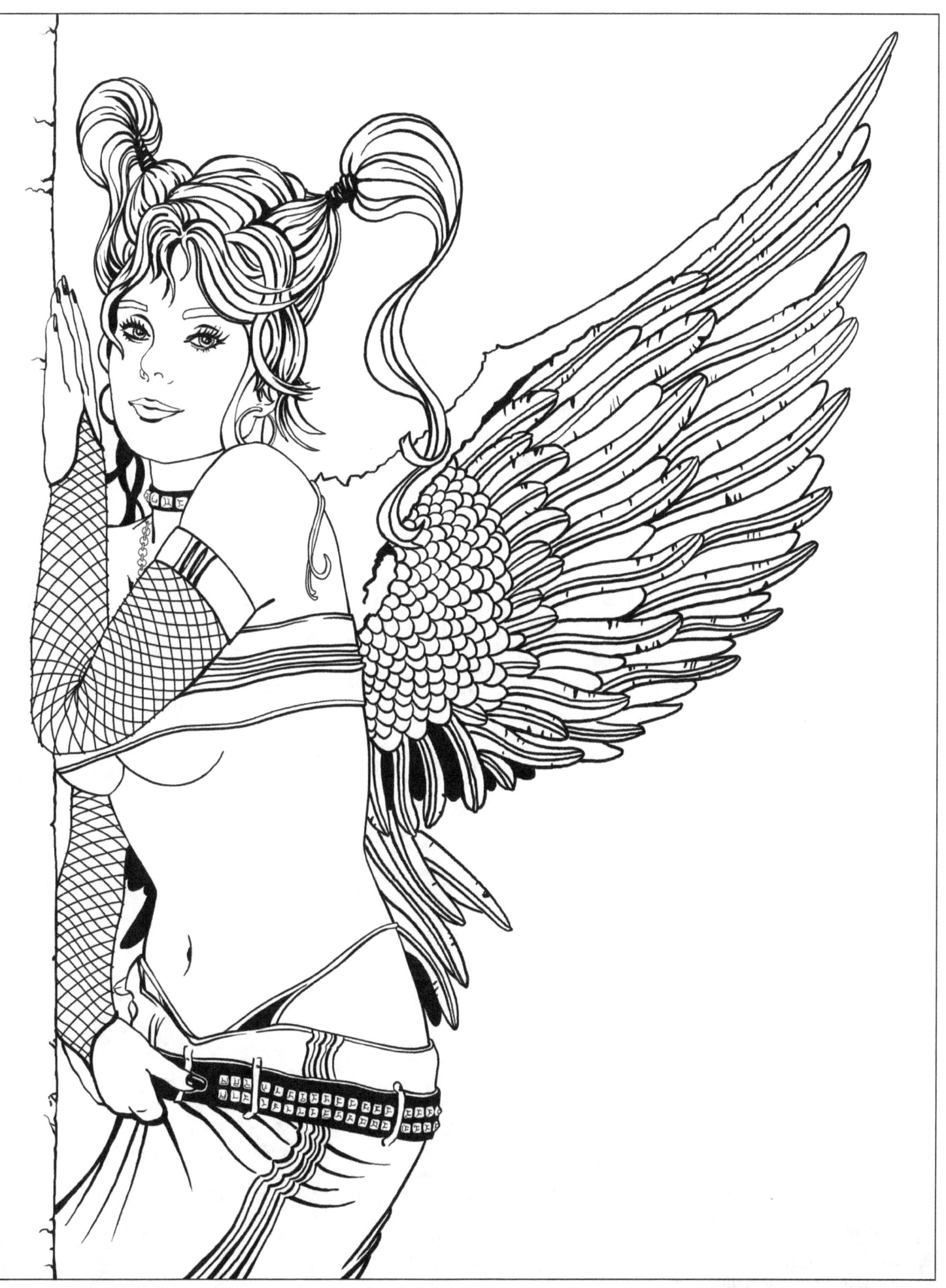

www.ingramcontent.com/pod-product-compliance
Lightning Source LLC
Chambersburg PA
CBHW081255180526
45170CB00007B/2436